# Sunday School Specials

By Lois Keffer

**Group** *Books*

Loveland, Colorado

# Dedication

To our wonderful friends at the St. Charles church
whose creativity and love of God opened new doors
of joy and learning.

## Sunday School Specials

Copyright © 1992 Lois Keffer

## Credits

Edited by Paul Woods
Designed by Dori Walker
Cover designed by Liz Howe
Illustrations by Raymond Medici

Scriptures quoted from The Youth Bible, New Century Version, copyright © 1991 by Word Publishing, Dallas, Texas 75039. Used by permission.

**Library of Congress Cataloging-in-Publication Data**
Keffer, Lois.
    Sunday school specials / by Lois Keffer.
        p.   cm.
    ISBN 1-55945-082-7
    1. Christian education—Textbooks for children. 2. Bible—Study and teaching. 3. Christian education of children. I. Title.
BV1561.K38   1992
268'.432—dc20
                91-36923
                CIP

15  14  13  12  11  10 9 8          03  02  01  00  99  98  97  96

Printed in the United States of America.

# Contents

## THE LESSONS

### TAKING RESPONSIBILITY FOR ...

#### My Relationship With God

#### My Feelings

3

## My Relationships With Others

# Introduction

Once upon a time there was a Christian education director who dreaded summer vacation. It's not that she objected to fun in the sun and that sort of thing—the problem was that when vacation arrived, Sunday school became exceedingly unpredictable. One week there would be eight kids in a class, and the next week there would be two. The following week somebody would bring 10 cousins, and kids would be hanging off the rafters. And, of course, the 10-cousin Sunday would be the day all the other teachers were out of town. What to do?

One day someone in the congregation said, "Let's put all the kids together and do some kind of creative Bible lesson with the whole group." And then a series of wonderful things began to happen. Kids began to look forward to Sunday school because they knew it wouldn't be the same old out-of-the-book stuff. Little kids liked getting lots of attention from big kids. And big kids liked helping out and being looked up to.

The teachers really got into it, too. Everyone signed up to teach one or two Sundays. The rest of the summer they could join an adult class or take some much needed R & R. In fact, the concept of combined classes went over so well the adults in the congregation got a little jealous. So she set up a couple of intergenerational lessons each summer  and let them join in.

"Why save these combined classes for summer?" the teachers asked. Why indeed? So she began using combined classes whenever holidays, absences or in-between-quarters Sundays presented a strategic dilemma.

The joyful, memorable learning experiences in those combined classes gave birth to the idea of *Sunday School Specials*. In this book you'll find a whole quarter's worth of creative, combined-class Bible lessons you can use in the summer or any time at all!

Each lesson contains an opening game or activity that grabs kids' attention and gets them tuned into the theme. You'll also find an interactive Bible story, a life-application activity and a reproducible handout that help kids apply what the Bible says to their own lives. And each lesson ends with a challenging, meaningful closing.

Within each lesson we'll let you know what to expect from kids of different ages, and we'll give you tips on how to get kids working together. And you'll find special ideas for gearing each Bible lesson to the needs of your kids. The hands-on, active-learning techniques will make it easy to capture and keep kids' interest. And you can be sure the Bible lessons they learn will stick with them for a long time.

You have in your hand a wonderful tool that can help you solve your Sunday dilemmas. So go ahead and try something new. We want to help you make your Sunday school special!

*Lois Keffer*

# Active Learning in Combined Classes

Research shows people remember most of what they do but only a small percentage of what they hear. Which means kids don't do their best learning sitting around a table talking! They need to be involved in lively activities that help bring home the truth of the lesson. Active learning involves teaching through experiences.

Students do things that help them understand important principles, messages and ideas. Active learning is a discovery process that helps students internalize the truth as it unfolds. Kids don't sit and listen as a teacher tells them what to think and believe—they find out for themselves.

Each active-learning experience is followed by questions that encourage kids to share their feelings about what just happened. Further discussion questions help kids interpret their feelings and decide how this truth affects their lives. The final part of each lesson challenges kids to decide what they'll do with what they've learned—how they'll apply it to their lives during the coming week.

How do kids feel about active learning? They love it! Sunday school becomes exciting, slightly unpredictable, and more relevant and life-changing than ever before. So put the table aside, gather your props and prepare for some unique and memorable learning experiences!

Active learning works beautifully in combined classes. When the group is playing a game or acting out a Bible story, kids of all ages can participate on an equal level. You don't need to worry about reading levels and writing skills.

Everyone gets a chance to make important contributions to class activities and discussions.

These simple classroom tips will help you get your combined class off to a smooth start:

● When kids form groups, aim for an equal balance of older and younger kids in each group. Encourage the older kids to act as coaches to help younger students get in the swing of each activity.

● In "pair-share," students work together with a partner. When it's time to report to the whole group, each person tells his or her partner's response. This simple technique teaches kids to listen and to cooperate with each other.

● If an activity calls for reading or writing, pair young non-readers with older kids who can lend their skills. Older kids enjoy the esteem-boost that comes with acting as a mentor, and younger kids appreciate getting special attention and broadening their skills.

● Don't worry too much about discussion going over the heads of younger students. They'll be stimulated by what they hear the older kids saying. You may be surprised to find some of the most insightful discussion literally coming "out of the mouths of babes."

● Make it a point to give everyone—not just academically and athletically gifted students—a chance to shine. Affirm kids for their cooperative attitudes when you see them working well together and encouraging each other.

● Keep in mind kids may give unexpected answers. That's okay. The answers given in parentheses after questions are simply suggestions of what kids *may* say, not the "right" answers. When kids give "wrong" answers, don't correct them. Say something like: "That's interesting. Let's look at it from another viewpoint." Then ask for ideas from other kids. If you correct kids' answers, most students will soon stop offering them.

# How to Get Started With Sunday School Specials

### Teaching Staff

When you combine Sunday school classes, teachers get a break! Teachers who would normally be teaching in your 4- to 12-year-old age groups may want to take turns. Or, ask teachers to sign up for the Sundays they'll be available to teach.

### Lesson Choice

The lessons in *Sunday School Specials* are grouped in three units, but each lesson is designed to stand on its own. You're not locked into doing the lessons in any particular order. Choose the topics that best suit the needs of your class. Two of the lessons contain suggestions for using an intergenerational approach—inviting parents and other adults in the congregation to join the class. You may want to schedule these lessons for special Sundays in your church calendar.

### Preparation

Each week you'll need to gather the easy-to-find props in the You'll Need section and photocopy the reproducible handouts. Add to that a careful read of the lesson and scripture passages, and you're ready to go!

# Time-Stuffers

What do you do when kids arrive 15 minutes early? When one group finishes before others do? When there's extra time after class is over? Get kids involved in a time-stuffer!

Each time-stuffer needs just one preparation—then it's ready to use whenever you're teaching these lessons. Choose from the following the time-stuffer that best appeals to the interests of your group, or set up all three.

### Prayer Line

You'll need two pieces of clothesline, bright-colored clothespins, paper, markers, 3×5 cards and string. Hang the two pieces of clothesline across a corner of the room. Clothespin a sign on one clothesline that reads, "Prayer Line." Clothespin a sign on the second clothesline that reads, "Praise Line." Tie string around a few markers and hang them from the clothesline at intervals. Encourage kids to write their prayer concerns on 3×5 cards and clothespin them to the Prayer Line. Take time to visit the Prayer Line as a class from time to time and pray about the requests. When a prayer is answered, students can write the answer on the back of the card and transfer the card to the Praise Line.

Tell kids they can add extra praises any time, even if it isn't something they prayed about!

### Group's Discover-It Bible Map™ Hunt

You'll need *Group's Discover-It Bible Map™*, 3×5 cards and markers. Hang *Group's Discover-It Bible Map™* on a classroom wall. Write challenging things for kids to find on separate 3×5 cards. For example, you might write, "What was the name of the mountain where Noah's ark came to rest?" or "How many camels can you find?"

When kids have a few minutes to fill, the map can give them a fun and interesting challenge and help them learn more about the Bible!

### Vacation Board

You'll need a cork board, picture postcards, push pins and palm trees cut from construction paper. Mount the cork board at a height that's easily accessible to your youngest class members. Decorate it with construction paper palm trees and a few scenic postcards.

Encourage kids to bring in postcards, brochures, photographs or drawings of places they travel to. Kids will have fun sharing their experiences and finding out about what their classmates have been doing.

# My Relationship
# With God

# Jesus, Our Shepherd

**1**

## LESSON AIM

To help kids understand Jesus wants to give us loving guidance and protection.

## OBJECTIVES

Kids will:
- realize Jesus is kind and loving, and he wants the best for them;
- understand Jesus can be close to them when they feel separated and lost;
- trust Jesus to guide them; and
- make a commitment to follow Jesus.

## BIBLE BASIS

**Psalm 23**

This psalm needs to be read from a sheep's point of view. Notice the sheep's delight in its wonderful shepherd. With the shepherd close by, the sheep had no fear—even though the canyons leading to the high grassy meadows were difficult to climb and full of predators.

Jesus welcomes this kind of total dependence and trust from us. Society teaches us to be strong and self-reliant, but scripture shows us we're truly strong and safe only when we're close to our good shepherd.

## YOU'LL NEED

- ❏ blindfolds
- ❏ an older girl to play Woolina
- ❏ a photocopy of "Woolina's Mask" (p. 20)
- ❏ scissors
- ❏ newsprint
- ❏ markers
- ❏ tape
- ❏ Bibles
- ❏ photocopies of the "Psalm-Pstarter" handout (p. 21)
- ❏ pencils

**John 10:1-15**

The sheep know the shepherd's voice, and he knows their names. What a wonderful assurance for kids to realize Jesus knows them each by name. The challenge is to learn to listen for his voice.

# UNDERSTANDING YOUR KIDS

Who doesn't remember at least one terrifying childhood experience that had to do with getting lost? First there's panic, then loneliness, then a sinking realization that there's probably little we can do to "get found." One lost-in-the-mall experience teaches kids the importance of sticking close to the person in charge.

Younger kids' biggest worry is they'll somehow be separated from their parents. They'll find comfort in knowing they have a good shepherd who cares for them and will always be with them, even when mom and dad are far away.

Older kids are anxious to grow up and assert their independence—that's natural and healthy. But they need to see true maturity means recognizing how much we need to rely on God. And it means following in the footsteps of our infinitely wise and loving good shepherd.

# The Lesson ATTENTION GRABBER

**Lost Sheep**

Use chairs to fence off one corner of the classroom as a "sheepfold." Make sure the fold has an entrance no bigger than the width of one chair. Explain that at night, sheep always come into the fold where they are protected from wolves, mountain lions and robbers.

Blindfold all of the children. One by one, take the blindfolded "sheep" to the "wilderness"—places far away from the fold. Take older kids farther into the wilderness than younger

14

kids—outside the class area. Make things more confusing by inventing twists and turns in your path as you lead them away. Have kids spin around three times and then try to find their way back to the fold.

If kids seem totally confused about how to get back to the fold, take them by the shoulders and gently turn them in the right direction. As you guide them, say: **This way, (name). This is the way to the fold.**

When everyone is gathered in the fold, have kids remove their blindfolds. Ask:

● **How did it feel trying to find your way back here?** (Scary; confusing; it was fun.)

● **How is this like what happens to you in real life when you get lost?** (I feel scared and don't know which way to go; somebody usually comes along to help.)

● **How is this different from really being lost?** (I knew I was really in Sunday school; all I had to do was pull off my blindfold.)

● **How did you feel when the shepherd came along to help you?** (I felt comforted; I liked hearing my name and being touched.)

● **How is Jesus like a shepherd to us?** (He knows all of us by name; he knows what's best for us and wants to help us and keep us safe.)

Say: **Today we're going to learn more about our good shepherd and about sheep. Tell me what you know about sheep.** Allow kids to respond. **You really know a lot! I'm going to introduce you to someone who will tell you more about sheep, and she ought to know because she is one! Please welcome my friend Woolina.**

Have the student who volunteered to play Woolina hold the mask (p. 20) in front of her face and read the Meet Woolina! story on page 16.

Have kids give Woolina a round of applause. Then ask:

● **What did Woolina say that surprised you?** (Sheep could fall over and not be able to get up; they can't smell water like other animals.)

● **Woolina thinks people need shepherds, too; why would people need a shepherd?** (People sometimes get sick and need help; people face big problems in life and need the help of someone wise and strong.)

● **What kind of shepherd do you think Woolina would like to have?** (Someone who is patient; strong; brave; knows where good food is.)

As kids give their answers to the last question, list them on a sheet of newsprint taped to the wall. Then ask:

● **What kind of shepherd would you like to have?**

## TEACHER TIP

If your class is mostly older kids, make the Lost Sheep activity more lively by adding a wolf. Blindfold the wolf and lead him or her farther from the fold than any of the sheep. The wolf howls when it tags a sheep, and then the sheep must play dead.

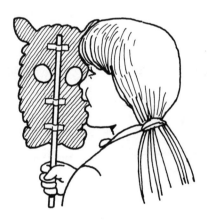

# Meet Woolina!

Baa!

My name is Woolina. I'm a sheep. A lot of people think sheep are really dumb. They're right! Turkeys may be a little dumber, but sheep are pretty dumb.

Do you know I could die of thirst with a pool of water just over the next hill? Sheep can't smell water like other animals can. I have no sense of direction. I couldn't find my way home if I had to. I don't even have enough sense to come in out of a storm!

I have no defenses at all. If a wolf or a mountain lion comes at me, I just stand there and wait to be eaten.

I'm not too smart about the way I eat, either. I've got really great teeth (show your teeth), and I can pull grass right up by the roots. My flock will often strip a field bare in just a few days and ruin the grazing there for years to come.

The most embarrassing thing about being a sheep is falling down and not being able to get up. If I roll over on my back too far I get stuck, and I just have to stay that way until help comes along.

You probably wonder how a dumb animal like me ever survives. Good question! The truth is, I depend on my shepherd for everything—food, water, shelter and protection. I wouldn't make it through a week without my shepherd.

I know you humans think you're a lot smarter than I am. But I've seen that humans need a lot of help, too. I think you're just pulling the wool over your own eyes. I don't want to be "baad," but it seems to me that you need a shepherd just as much as I do!

(Someone who understands me and cares about me; someone I can turn to when I'm scared.)

List these answers on the newsprint, as well.

Ask:

● **The Bible tells us about someone who wants to be our good shepherd; can anyone who is younger than 6 years old tell me who that is?** (Jesus.)

Say: **Let's see how this good shepherd compares to the list we've made here.**

# BIBLE STUDY

**The Good Shepherd (Psalm 23; John 10:1-15)**

Gather all the kids into the fold. Ask for one volunteer to be a robber and one to be a wolf. The rest of the kids will be sheep. Whenever you mention the word "shepherd," all the sheep are to smile and say "baa!" But the robber and wolf are to turn around and hide their faces. Tell kids to listen carefully for their parts in the Bible story and to do exactly what it says.

Read John 10:1-15 in your best storytelling manner. Be sure to use a version of the Bible kids will easily understand. Emphasize "shepherd" so kids can catch their cues.

After the story, have kids sit in a circle.

Ask:

● **What did you like best about the good shepherd?** (I like it that he knows all the sheep by name; I like him for protecting the sheep from wolves and robbers.)

● **What would it feel like to have a shepherd like that?** (Safe; happy.)

● **How is Jesus like the good shepherd in this story?** (He cares for us and gives us the things we need; he gave his life for us.)

● **In the story, the good shepherd protected the sheep from wolves and robbers. What kinds of scary things can Jesus help us face today?** (Getting separated from mom or dad; facing mean kids at school; getting sick.)

● **How is having Jesus in your life like having a good shepherd?** (I can turn to him in prayer when I feel scared or kids are bugging me.)

Now have kids turn to Psalm 23. Little ones who can't read yet will enjoy looking on with older readers.

Say: **Today we're going to do something fun and different with this psalm.**

Have kids form six groups. A group can be as few as one or two kids. Include older and younger kids in each group.

Assign each of the six groups one verse of Psalm 23, and have them make up their own sign language to tell what the verse says. Encourage kids to use their whole bodies to express the meanings of their verses.

Allow a couple of minutes for kids to plan. Then bring everyone together, and line up the groups in verse order. Read the psalm aloud and have kids perform their verses.

Ask:

● **How did you feel as you did the motions you made up?** (Happy; excited.)

● **How does performing this psalm make you feel about Jesus?** (It makes me love him; I want to stay close to him; it makes me glad there's someone strong who will always be there for me.)

Say: **I hope you'll remember the good feelings you get from this psalm. Also remember the psalm doesn't promise that nothing scary will ever happen to us. But it does promise our good shepherd will be with us through good times and bad times, and he will always make things turn out right in the end.**

# LIFE APPLICATION

**Psalms for the Shepherd**

Give kids each a photocopy of the "Psalm-Pstarter" handout (p. 21) and a pencil.

Say: **You can write a psalm of your own and tell Jesus how you feel about him. We'll be using the sheep pictures later.**

Circulate among kids as they're working, giving them ideas and encouragement, and helping those who are having trouble. Have kids share their finished psalms. Praise them for the love they expressed and for their creativity.

**Jesus' Flock**

Draw kids' attention to the characteristics of a good shepherd that they listed on the newsprint earlier. Let young readers raise their hands if they can read a word on the list. Have them come up individually, point to a word and read it.

For each characteristic ask:

● **Is Jesus like this? Why or why not?**

When you've been through the whole list, ask the class:

● **Do you want Jesus to be your shepherd? Why or why not?**

Ask a 7- or 8-year-old to come up and draw a picture of Jesus on a sheet of newsprint. Have an older child title the picture "Our Good Shepherd." Give kids each a pair of scissors and a pencil. Then have everyone cut out one of the sheep from their "Psalm-Pstarter" handouts.

Say: **Write your name on your sheep. Then bring it up here and tape it on the picture close to Jesus.**

Pass out strips of tape as kids bring up their sheep. When the "flock" has been assembled on the newsprint, ask:

● **What can you do to stay close to the good shepherd this week?** (Sing songs that remind me of Jesus; pray; read the Bible or listen to Bible stories; ask Jesus to be with me in scary times.)

Have kids each cut out the other sheep from the "Psalm-Pstarter" handout and write on it one thing they'll do to stay close to Jesus this week. Younger kids can draw instead of write. Encourage kids to show their sheep to their parents and discuss their plans for staying close to the good shepherd.

# CLOSING

**Thanks to the Shepherd**

Have kids sing the simple round "The Lord Is My Shepherd" or another simple song about Jesus. Then have them huddle for a closing prayer, thanking Jesus for caring for them and being their good shepherd.

# WOOLINA'S MASK

Cut out this mask and the holes for the eyes. You may want to glue the mask to cardboard and tape a ruler or dowel on the back for a handle.

Write your own psalm by completing these sentences.

Because the Lord is . . .

I will never . . .

Lord, you are . . .

Thank you, for I will always . . .

# 2 God's Gift of Forgiveness

## YOU'LL NEED

- ❑ six 2-liter bottles
- ❑ several plastic holders from six-packs of soft drinks
- ❑ scissors
- ❑ masking tape
- ❑ three nickels per child
- ❑ paper
- ❑ pencils
- ❑ Bibles
- ❑ photocopies of the "Forgiveness Is a Two-Way Street" handout (p. 28)
- ❑ ribbon

You'll also need three grocery bags with the following items in them:

- ❑ grocery bag 1: a 3×5 card with Luke 15:11-14 written on it, a stack of play money and a backpack;
- ❑ grocery bag 2: a 3×5 card with Luke 15:15-20 written on it, a dirty work shirt and a plastic container with food scraps in it; and
- ❑ grocery bag 3: a 3×5 card with Luke 15:21-24 written on it, a bathrobe, a pair of men's sandals and a ring made of aluminum foil.

## LESSON AIM

To help kids realize the importance of both receiving God's gift of forgiveness and passing it on to others.

## OBJECTIVES

Kids will:
- experience grace by getting prizes without earning them;
- act out the story of the lost son receiving forgiveness from his father;
- name things for which they have been forgiven; and
- be willing to pass on forgiveness to others.

## BIBLE BASIS

**Luke 15:11-32**

The parable of the prodigal son illustrates forgiveness at its best—and worst. The irresponsible young man who stars in this story did things that were unthinkable in a family of that day. He took his inheritance before his father's death; he blew the money on selfish, wild living; and then proceeded to live the lowest life as a pig farmer. Yet, in spite of it all, the father freely offered forgiveness and acceptance when the repentant son found his way home. God still offers that same unconditional forgiveness to anyone who will "come home" to him today.

### Matthew 6:14-15

Because God so freely forgives us, we in turn are to forgive others. The concept of forgiving so we can be forgiven isn't terribly comfortable for kids or adults. We want to be forgiven, and then—like the older brother in the story—decide for ourselves whether others deserve our forgiveness. Jesus' challenge reminds us forgiving others isn't optional—it's part of his call to discipleship.

# UNDERSTANDING YOUR KIDS

It's been said that when it comes to forgiveness, kids ought to be teaching adults. One of the world's most amazing sights is two best buddies walking side by side after a shouting match just moments before. Long-lasting grudges and feuds seldom develop among children unless the conflict is fueled by adults. This lesson capitalizes on the forgiving nature of the younger generation, and on kids' sincere desire for simple, harmonious relationships.

This forgiving nature is balanced by a strong sense of justice, especially in older kids. They, like the older brother in the prodigal son story, want to see "bad guys" get what they've got coming. The challenge here is to help kids see we're all sinners adopted into God's family by his grace. This grace is free to anyone, any time. And since God freely gives it to us, he expects us to pass it on to others.

Secular culture gives kids a strong message—revenge and pay-backs feel good. We need to show them forgiveness feels better.

# The Lesson

## ATTENTION GRABBER

**No-Loss Toss**

Set up a ringtoss game with six 2-liter bottles arranged in a triangle like bowling pins. Cut apart several plastic rings that hold six-packs of soft drinks together. Kids will try to toss the rings over the necks of the bottles.

Use masking tape to mark a "toss line" for younger kids about 3 feet back from the bottles. Mark a second line a couple of feet farther away for older kids.

Say: **We're going to play a ringtoss game. For every ring you land over the neck of a bottle, I'll give you a nickel.**

Give kids each three tries, and award a nickel for each try whether the ring lands on a bottle or not. If kids are puzzled by your generosity, just ignore them and keep the game going. Have the group cheer for the efforts of every player.

After the game, ask:

● **What was strange about this game?** (We kept getting nickels whether we earned them or not.)

● **How did you feel about getting nickels when you messed up and didn't really earn them?** (Like I didn't deserve them; I thought it was great.)

Ask the kids who actually landed the rings on the bottles:

● **How did you feel when you landed the rings but ended up getting the same prize as people who didn't land any? Explain.** (It made me mad because I earned a prize and the others didn't; I felt kind of cheated.)

● **How is getting a prize when you didn't earn it like receiving forgiveness when you mess up in real life?** (I don't really deserve what I'm getting.)

Say: **The amazing and wonderful thing is that no matter how many times we mess up in life, God is always willing to give us his free gift of forgiveness. With God, it doesn't matter if we're winners or losers, or how many times we've blown it. He offers us forgiveness, no matter what.**

**Today we're going to participate in a story Jesus told about somebody who messed up big time. In fact, there wasn't a whole lot more he could have done wrong. Let's see how things turned out for him.**

24

**A Father Forgives (Luke 15:11-32)**

Give kids each a sheet of paper and a pencil. Say: **To set the stage for our Bible study, I want you to create an imaginary bedroom for yourself, and you can have anything in it you want. You've got two minutes to draw or write what you'd want in your room. Go!**

Call time after two minutes. Then have kids find partners. Encourage older kids to pair up with younger ones.

Say: **You now have one minute to find out what your partner put in his or her room. Then I'm going to ask each of you to tell about your partner's room.**

Bring everyone together for the pair-share. After kids have told about their partners' ideal rooms, ask:

● **How did it feel to put together your own room? Explain.** (Awesome, I wish I could really have a room like this.)

● **Do you think having a room like that would really make you happy? Why or why not?** (Sure, it would be great to have all that stuff; not really, things can't give me love no matter how neat they are.)

Say: **Our story today is about a kid who had it all. He had the best room a Bible-time kid could have. He had a neat family, and his dad was a wealthy landowner. But all this wasn't enough.**

**That's all I'm going to tell you of the story. The rest is up to you. Let's form three groups to tell the rest of the story. I have a bag of things for each group to use. In your groups, read your scripture and then decide how to use the things in your bag to tell the story to the rest of the class.**

Give groups each one grocery bag containing the following items:

Group 1: a 3×5 card with Luke 15:11-14 written on it, a stack of play money and a backpack.

Group 2: a 3×5 card with Luke 15:15-20 written on it, a dirty work shirt and a plastic container with food scraps in it.

Group 3: a 3×5 card with Luke 15:21-24 written on it, a bathrobe, a pair of men's sandals and a ring made of aluminum foil.

Allow about three minutes for Bible study and planning; then have groups present their portions of the Bible story.

After the presentations, ask:

● **How did it feel to take off with all that money in**

## TEACHER TIP

If you have older kids who can take the lead in creating skits to tell the story, encourage them to do so. An alternate approach is to let kids act out the story as you read it straight from the Bible.

## TEACHER TIP

Encourage kids to add lots of sound effects. (They'll love making pig noises!) Don't be afraid to let kids' creativity flow—you can easily refocus the class by using a pre-arranged attention-getting signal (flashing the lights or having kids raise their hands in response to your raised hand).

your hands? Explain. (Cool, I know just how I'd spend it.)

● **How did it feel to put on the dirty shirt and smell the food scraps? Explain.** (Yucky, I'd never do that.)

● **How did it feel to be welcomed home with a big hug and new clothes?** (Scary at first, but then really good.)

● **How were those feelings like feelings you've had when someone has forgiven you?** Encourage kids to share their personal experiences. You might begin by telling about a time when you received forgiveness.

Then say: **Guess what? That isn't the end of the story.** Read aloud Luke 15:25-32.

Ask:

● **Why was the older brother feeling angry?** (Because he stayed home and worked hard, but his younger brother was getting all the attention.)

● **Do you think the older brother had a right to feel that way? Why or why not?** (Yes, the younger brother didn't deserve a party; no, the father loved both his sons, but was especially glad to have the younger one home again.)

● **How is the father giving a party for his long-lost son similar to how God treats people who ask him for forgiveness?** (No matter how much people sin and mess up their lives, God is always ready to forgive them.)

Say: **Sometimes we might think—like the older brother did—that a person doesn't deserve to be forgiven. But God wants us to always be loving and forgiving, just like he is. Let's look at a Bible verse that explains how God's forgiveness works.**

# LIFE APPLICATION

**Both Sides of the Street**

Give kids each a photocopy of the "Forgiveness Is a Two-Way Street" handout (p. 28) and a pencil.

Have a volunteer read aloud Matthew 6:14-15 from the handout.

Ask:

● **How important is it to forgive others?** (Pretty important; God says he won't forgive us unless we do.)

● **How is forgiveness like a two-way street?** (It goes both ways—we receive it and give it.)

Say: **On one side of the street, draw or write things God has forgiven you for. On the other side, draw or write things you may need to forgive others for.**

After kids have finished, ask:

● **How does it feel to look at the list of things God has forgiven you for?** (It makes me feel glad that God is so loving; it makes me wish I hadn't blown it so often.)

● **How does it feel to look at the list of things you need to forgive other people for?** (Angry; I think it will be hard to do.)

● **Does seeing the two lists side by side make it easier to forgive others? Why or why not?** (No, I still feel mad when people are mean to me; yes, I realize if God can forgive me for all those things, then I can forgive others.)

# COMMITMENT

### A Gift From God

Form pairs. Give students each a 2-foot length of ribbon. Have kids each fold up their handout and wrap it with their ribbon. Have partners work together to tie bows.

Say: **This little package is to remind you forgiveness is a gift from God—a gift he wants you to pass on to others.**

Encourage kids to show their gifts to their parents and to discuss what they wrote or drew.

# CLOSING

### Forgiveness Circle

Form circles of about eight and join a circle yourself. Have kids stand close together with their arms extended forward and hands palms up, touching in the center, as if they're about to receive a large gift. Older kids and adults may need to kneel to touch hands with younger children. Pray a simple prayer, thanking God for the gift of forgiveness and asking for his help in passing it on to others.

# FORGIVENESS IS A 2-WAY STREET

On one side of the street, draw or write things God has forgiven you for. On the other side of the street, draw or write things you need to forgive others for.

"Yes, if you forgive others for their sins, your Father in heaven will also forgive you for your sins. But if you don't forgive others, your Father in heaven will not forgive your sins" Matthew 6:14-15.

# How God Talks to Us

**3**

## LESSON AIM

To help kids open themselves to God through Bible reading and prayer.

## OBJECTIVES

Kids will:
- come to see the Bible as God's personal word to them;
- present commercials about the benefits of God's Word;
- practice listening prayers; and
- plan a personal quiet time.

## BIBLE BASIS

**Psalm 119:97-104**

Psalm 119 is unique in several ways. It's the longest chapter in scripture, and it's also an acrostic. Each stanza starts with one of the 22 letters of the Hebrew alphabet. But most significant is this psalm's unique theme of praise to God for his Word. Unlike other psalms that focus on what God has done and is doing, Psalm 119 gives praise to God's Word and the help and guidance it brings to our lives.

**1 Samuel 3:2-11**

The remarkable thing about this familiar story is God bypassed a priest and gave a message of great importance to a child. It's never too early for children to learn to listen for God's voice—and to obey it.

## YOU'LL NEED

- ❑ a honeycomb or jar of honey
- ❑ graham crackers
- ❑ Bibles
- ❑ plastic knives
- ❑ paper plates
- ❑ damp washcloths
- ❑ a large white onion
- ❑ hexagons cut from yellow construction paper
- ❑ pencils
- ❑ tape
- ❑ photocopies of the "I'm Listening, Lord" mini-journal (p. 36)

# UNDERSTANDING YOUR KIDS

We are currently raising what some call the "media generation." Kids are constantly bombarded with auditory and visual stimuli. Just watch 15 minutes of Saturday-morning television sometime, and see if you can keep pace with everything that's happening!

The challenge for us as Christian teachers is to get kids to see spending a few quiet moments with God each day can make a tremendous difference in their lives. With no commercials, jingles or two-for-one offers to entice them, kids need to see there's eternal hope, help and unending love just waiting to be tapped.

Younger kids will benefit from your making available a variety of Bible-story books and tapes for them to borrow. Then they can follow through on the principles they'll learn in this session.

Older kids need concrete guidance about how and when to approach daily Bible study and prayer. Many Christian educators direct upper-elementary kids to the books of Psalms and James for their first ventures into independent Bible study. The "I'm Listening, Lord" mini-journal will be an excellent tool to help your kids get started with a daily quiet time.

# The Lesson ATTENTION GRABBER

**Listen Up**

Ask for a volunteer to leave the room. Choose an older student who will reliably follow your directions. When the volunteer has left, show the rest of the kids where you're going to hide the honey and graham crackers.

Say: **When (name) comes back into the room, you're going to try to guide (him or her) to the honey and graham crackers by giving the clues "hot" and "cold." No fair moving or pointing or giving any other clues. If (name) finds the honey and graham crackers within 30** seconds, everyone gets to share them.

Slip into the hall with the volunteer. Quickly explain he or she is just to stroll around the classroom and completely ignore the clues the other kids are giving.

Bring the volunteer back into the classroom.

Say: **Is everybody ready? The 30 seconds starts . . . now!**

Notify kids when you're down to 20 and 15 seconds. Then as their excitement mounts, count down the seconds from 10 to zero. Have everyone, including your volunteer, sit down. Warn kids that the location of the honey and graham crackers must still be kept secret.

Ask:

● **How did you feel as (name) ignored your clues? Explain.** (Frustrated, I felt like I had to yell louder.)

● **What's so bad about (name) not paying attention to what you were saying?** (Now we don't get the honey and graham crackers.)

● **How is (name) ignoring your directions like people who live their lives without paying any attention to what God has to say to them?** (They miss out on good things, too.)

Say: **Okay, let's play this game again. This time, (name), pay attention to the clues the kids are giving you.**

Let the kids call out "hot" and "cold" again to lead the volunteer to the honey and graham crackers. Have everyone give the volunteer a big round of applause. Then gather kids in a circle, place the honey and graham crackers in the center and ask:

● **How did you feel as (name) got closer and closer to the honey and graham crackers?** (Happy; excited.)

● **How is that like being tuned in to what God has to say to you?** (It's exciting; neat things happen to us.)

● **What are some ways we can tune in to God?** (Reading the Bible; praying.)

Say: **We're going to eat the honey and graham crackers in just a minute, but first, let's look at something the Bible says.**

## TEACHER TIP

If kids in your class are younger or especially excitable, you might have them sit on their hands before bringing the volunteer back into the room.

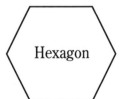

Hexagon

**Tuning In to God**
**(1 Samuel 3:2-11; Psalm 119:97-104)**

Have kids turn their Bibles to Psalm 119:97-104. Have older kids read the psalm aloud, each reading one verse.

After the reading, bring out plastic knives and paper plates. If you were able to obtain a honeycomb, let kids examine it. Some kids may be able to explain how and why the bees construct the honeycomb.

Have kids each dip a knife into the honey and spread the honey onto a graham cracker.

As kids are enjoying their snacks, say: **Oh no! I forgot! Would anyone rather have this for a treat?** Pull out a big white onion.

Kids will probably laugh as they assure you they'd rather have the honey and graham crackers.

Ask:

● **What's so good about honey?** (It's sweet; it's good for you.)

● **How is learning what the Bible says like eating honey?** (It's good and good for us; we don't want to stop.)

● **Why did the psalm writer compare reading the Bible to eating honey? Why didn't he compare it to eating an onion?** (Honey is a delicious treat; it's sweet and rich and good, like God's Word; onions are hot and give you bad breath.)

● **What good things do you get from honey?** (Energy; vitamins.)

● **What good things do you get from reading the Bible?** (I learn about God's love; I get guidance for my life; I get comfort when I'm feeling sad.)

Pass out pencils. Choose kids to write (or draw symbols of) these responses on yellow construction paper hexagons and tape them to the wall. Explain that the hexagons represent the honey and the honeycomb the psalm writer was talking about.

Say: **That's pretty sweet stuff! Let's look back at this psalm for a minute.**

Ask:

● **What does the psalm writer say reading God's Word does for him?** (It makes him wiser than his enemies; it gives him understanding; it keeps him from doing evil.)

Have kids write or draw these responses on yellow hexagons and add them to the honeycomb wall.

Say: **God talks to us through his Word. The Bible is like a personal letter written to each one of us. You know how fun it is to get letters in the mail—imagine getting a letter from God! You'd want to read it every day, over and over again. And I hope you will.**

**God talks to us in other ways, too—especially through prayer.**

Ask:

● **What do you pray about when you pray?** (I thank God for the things he gives me; I ask him for things I need; I ask him to take care of my friends and family.)

Say: **Did you ever think of listening to God in prayer? Let's learn about someone in the Bible who listened to God—someone who may have been close to your age.**

Have older kids open their Bibles to 1 Samuel 3:2-11. Choose students to read the parts of the narrator, Samuel, God and Eli. Be ready to signal the characters as their turns come to read. Position four chairs as corners of a big square. Turn down the lights, if possible, to fit the setting of the story. Have the readers sit on the chairs, with all the other kids on the floor in the middle.

When everyone is in place, introduce the story this way:

**Samuel was a boy whose mother sent him to serve the Lord when he was still very young. He was raised by an old priest named Eli. So Samuel grew up in the temple. This story happened late one night. Sh! It's very dark in the temple ... and very quiet ... and young Samuel is just about to fall asleep.**

Signal the readers to begin.

After the reading, explain that God went on to tell Samuel how the family of Eli would be punished for breaking God's laws.

Then ask:

● **Who did Samuel think was calling him at first?** (Eli, the old priest.)

● **Why was he confused about who was calling him?** (He'd never heard God talking to him before.)

● **Why is nighttime a good time to listen to God?** (Because everything is still and quiet; nothing else is grabbing our attention.)

● **When are other times you can listen for God?** (When I'm riding the school bus; when I'm in church; when I'm waiting in line at lunch.)

Say: **Because Samuel was listening, God gave him a big, important job to do. Samuel became the leader of the whole nation of Israel. But it's important to remember Samuel didn't understand what God was doing right**

## TEACHER TIP

Seat yourself among the kids in the middle. Being in the middle of a group of kids instead of in front of them helps you keep control and their attention in a storytelling situation.

at first. He had to turn to an older friend for guidance.

You may need to do that, too. God doesn't often speak to people in an out-loud voice. Sometimes, he speaks to us more silently, and we may need to ask other people for help in deciding whether it's really God talking to us.

Ask:

● **Who are some people who could help you understand when God is talking to you?** (Parents; the pastor; Sunday school teachers.)

● **Do you think God has time to talk to kids? Why or why not?** (Sure, he talked to Samuel; no, he's too busy.)

● **Do you think kids have time to listen to God? Why or why not?** (No, sometimes we're too busy; yes, we should always pray and listen.)

Say: **God has wonderful things in store for people who are willing to listen to him and to obey, and it doesn't make any difference if you're young, old or in between! The important thing is that you take time to tune in to God.**

## LIFE APPLICATION

**All the Good Things**

Say: **Speaking of tuning in, I know you're all experts in commercials. How many commercials would you guess you see on television in one week?** Allow kids to guess. **Now is your chance to make a commercial about something really important.**

Form two groups. Have one group plan a commercial about the good things that come from reading the Bible. Have the other group plan a commercial about the benefits of listening to God. Appoint a director for each group. Encourage the directors to plan commercials where the younger kids can play an important part.

Allow time for the groups to plan and rehearse their commercials. Then have them perform for each other.

## TEACHER TIP

Kids love to perform for a camera. If you bring a video camera to tape the finished commercials, kids are sure to participate with enthusiasm. Parents would appreciate viewing their kids' efforts after class.

**Time With God**

Say: **I'm glad you're all excited about looking for God's guidance. I have a little journal for each of you that will help you keep praying and reading your Bible each day.**

Give kids each a photocopy of the "I'm Listening, Lord" mini-journal (p. 36) and a pencil. Show kids how to fold the journal and help younger kids write their names on the front.

Explain that the journal has a place where kids can write each day what they read, what they prayed about and what they thought about after reading the Bible and praying.

Explain to kids who don't yet have reading and writing skills that they can look at a Bible-story book each day and draw pictures of the Bible story in their journals. They can also draw pictures of the things they pray about and of how they feel after being quiet with God for a while.

Ask:

● **When would be a good time for you to have your quiet time with God each day?** Ask kids to respond individually, and then fill in the hands of the clock to show the time they named. Encourage kids to think of this time as an appointment with someone who loves them very much.

**Practicing Prayer**

Say: **Now we're going to take some time to pray and to listen to God. We're all going to bow our heads. I'm going to pray a short prayer, and then we'll all be quiet for a few moments. Then I'll finish the prayer.**

**Dear Lord, thank you for guiding us to good things in your Word. Thank you for talking to us when we take time to listen. Help us think about what we've learned today and listen to you right now.** Pause for a few seconds. **Help us to keep tuning in to you each day. In Jesus' name, amen.**

WHAT I PRAYED ABOUT

WHAT I READ

DATE

WHAT I THOUGHT ABOUT

# I'm LISTENING LORD

## MINI-JOURNAL

MY QUIET TIME:

NAME: _____

"Your promises are sweet to me, sweeter than honey in my mouth!" Psalm 119:103.

# The Talent Trap

**4**

## LESSON AIM

To help kids view their talents as gifts from God that are to be used to serve him.

## OBJECTIVES

Kids will:
- recognize the drawbacks of bragging;
- learn to take healthy pride in what they do;
- affirm the talents they see in one another; and
- dedicate their own talents to God's service.

## BIBLE BASIS

**Matthew 21:1-9**

Jesus' choice of a small donkey to ride into Jerusalem was symbolic of his attitude. He was not coming as a conqueror on a great white horse but in peace and humility. What a contrast to the leaders of his day—and for that matter—to our leaders today.

Leadership philosophy today teaches that if you want to be a leader, you must demonstrate power and aggressiveness in the way you dress, speak and conduct your relationships. On Palm Sunday Jesus literally had it all, but he chose to submit to the will of the Father. The world says take all you can get; Jesus' example is to give it all away.

## YOU'LL NEED

- ❏ Bibles
- ❏ self-stick notes
- ❏ marker
- ❏ photocopies of the "Decoration Celebration" handout (p. 45)
- ❏ pencils
- ❏ confetti

**Philippians 2:3-4**

"When you do things, do not let selfishness or pride be your guide. Instead, be humble and give more honor to others than to yourselves." Talk about contrast to today's philosophies of leadership! You could never find that recommendation in today's self-help leadership books. But Paul says our example is not the world, but Jesus Christ. Humility such as Jesus demonstrates means recognizing God as the author of our talents, being submissive to his will and recognizing that others have worth in God's eyes—just as we do.

# UNDERSTANDING YOUR KIDS

Bragging is a nearly universal problem with kids. "My bike is better than yours." "My grandpa gives me 50 dollars for my birthday every year." "My music teacher says I'm one of her most talented students." Can't you just hear them? Bragging is a temporary and unsatisfactory solution for a sagging self-image. Kids need to see bragging does exactly the opposite of what they hope it will do: It hurts them in the eyes of others instead of building them up.

This lesson helps kids see that whatever they do that is worthy of praise is a gift of God. Since God is the source of what we have and what we are, the honor and praise should go to him.

Younger kids with rapidly developing skills are justified in taking pride in their accomplishments. But they can learn not to put down others' efforts to build up their own.

Older kids with their more developed abilities can express appreciation to God for the talents he's given them. And, they can dedicate those talents to God's service.

**Strange and Wonderful Talent Show**

Say: **I've noticed what a unique and talented bunch of kids you are. So today I'm going to give you a chance to show off some of your talents. We're going to begin class with a strange and wonderful talent show.**

Form four groups. Create a good mix of younger and older kids in each group. Send groups each to one of the four corners of the room. Explain that you'll come around and tell each group what it's supposed to do for the talent show.

Give the following assignments:

Group 1: Each student will do a different animal imitation; but they'll all do them at the same time.

Group 2: Kids will each make the strangest face they can.

Group 3: Kids will each try to stick out their tongue and touch the tip of their nose.

Group 4: Kids will stand in a line and try to rub their tummies and pat their heads at the same time.

Give kids about one minute to get themselves organized. Then have the groups take turns performing. Make sure each group gets a hearty round of applause for its efforts.

After the talent show, ask:

● **What was strange about this talent show?** (You made us do weird things; we were just being silly.)

● **How did you feel about doing the silly things I asked you to do?** (Embarrassed; it was fun.)

● **How was this like a real talent show?** (We had to stand in front of people and do something; people clapped for us.)

● **How was it different?** (We didn't have a chance to do things we're really good at.)

● **What kinds of things do you like to do in front of other people?** Kids' answers will vary.

● **How do you feel when people clap for you or say you did a great job? Explain.** (Great, it makes me want to do more.)

● **Is it okay to feel good about your accomplishments? Why or why not?** (Yes, as long as you don't make a big deal to other people; no, we shouldn't be proud.)

Say: **It's good to work hard and feel good about what**

you can do. But we get into problems if we get carried away with how great we are or if we start bragging about being better than other people. Today we're going to see how that happened in an imaginary story based on a Bible story.

## BIBLE STUDY

**To Brag or Not to Brag**
**(Matthew 21:1-9; Philippians 2:3-4)**

Have kids open their Bibles to Matthew 21:1-9 and take turns reading verses aloud. Or, you can ask kids to tell you the story of Jesus entering Jerusalem on Palm Sunday.

Say: **Today we're going to find out what the mother donkey in this story might have been thinking. But I need your help to tell the story.**

Practice each of these cues and responses with the kids:

● **Whenever I say "mother donkey," the girls go "heehaw."**

● **Whenever I say "colt," the boys make donkey ears with their hands.**

● **Whenever I say "crowd," bump your shoulders together.**

● **Whenever I say "Jesus," wave your arms and shout "hosanna!"**

● **Whenever I say "disciples," everybody in the second grade and up count to 12 as fast as you can.**

Then say: **Ready? Here we go with the story, The Proud Donkey.**

Read aloud The Proud Donkey story on page 41. Pause after each underlined word to let kids do their actions.

Ask:

● **The mother donkey has a problem; what is it?** (She was silly; the crowd was praising Jesus, not the colt.)

● **How could she have gotten so mixed up?** (She was so proud of her colt, she didn't even notice what the crowd was really saying.)

● **Who really was the important person in this story?** (Jesus.)

● **If you could talk to the mother donkey, what would you tell her?** (You silly donkey—they're praising Jesus, not your colt; quit bragging!)

Say: **Of course we know animals can't really think or behave like that. But have you ever seen people behave**

---

Read aloud The Proud Donkey story on page 41.

## TEACHER TIP

Younger children may know the story well and would appreciate this opportunity to shine in front of the older kids. Help them tell the story by asking questions and prompting them.

## TEACHER TIP

Older kids can easily handle five cues and responses. If your class is mostly younger children, you may wish to eliminate one or two of the responses so kids don't get confused.

# The Proud Donkey

Once upon a time in the faraway village of Bethphage, there lived a mother donkey and her little colt. The mother donkey was proud of her little colt. She was sure he was the most handsome little colt any mother donkey had ever had. He would surely fetch a fine price for her master, for the little colt was just now big enough to ride.

One day two of Jesus' disciples came to the house. They walked right up to the little colt, untied him, untied the mother donkey, and began to lead them away.

The master stopped them. "Why are you leading this colt away?" he asked.

"The Lord needs him," the disciples answered.

The master smiled and nodded, and sent them on their way.

The mother donkey was thrilled. "I knew it! I knew it!" she thought. "I knew some important person would spot my colt. He is truly the most handsome colt that ever walked the roads of Judea."

The mother donkey was very glad the disciples let her come along. She wanted to see her son in his moment of glory!

The disciples brought the colt to a man they called Jesus. Jesus spoke kindly, and his hands were gentle on the reins. "See what a good little colt I've raised," the mother donkey gloated as the little group started down the road to Jerusalem. "He's not giving that kind man Jesus any trouble at all."

As the group of travelers drew closer to Jerusalem, a strange thing began to happen. A crowd of people began to follow them. It was a happy, singing crowd. They were so happy to see the handsome young colt, they began to shout his praises. "Hosanna!" they cried. The mother donkey's heart swelled with pride as she followed behind. "I knew he would be great," she sighed. Then, wonder of wonders, the crowd began to cut palm branches and lay them in the path of the colt. All around them, people in the crowd were shouting and dancing and praising God for the wonderful colt. "That nice man Jesus must feel very honored to ride such a fine animal," thought the proud mother donkey. "Has any animal ever been so honored?"

Down through the streets of Jerusalem they paraded. The colt and the mother donkey stepped very proudly, for all along the way the crowd kept singing their praises.

like that proud mother donkey? Sometimes people are so proud and stuck-up and boastful, they're not very nice to be around. Let's see what kind of people God wants us to be.

Have kids turn to Philippians 2:3-4. Ask a volunteer to read it aloud.

Say: **God doesn't want us to go around bragging or putting other people down. He wants us to thank him for our abilities and to praise the abilities we see in others. To show you what I mean, let's do some "pop-up" answers.**

Explain that you're going to read some statements. For each statement, you'll say: **Pop up if you have a proud, boastful answer.** After kids have popped up and given proud, boastful answers, you'll say: **Pop up if you have a nicer, thoughtful answer.** Allow kids to respond both ways before moving to the next statement.

Here are the statements:

● **That was a beautiful solo you sang in church. You have such a nice voice!**

● **I heard you got an A from Mrs. Altman. She's a really hard teacher.**

● **Did you draw that? I can't believe you're such a good artist!**

After kids give their pop-up answers, ask:

● **How did you feel when you heard the bragging answers?** (I didn't like the person; I would never give them another compliment.)

● **How did you feel when you heard the nicer answers?** (She was a really nice person; it was fun to give the compliment.)

Say: **Sometimes it's easy to brag, even when people give us compliments. But God wants us to build up other people—not ourselves. So let's practice doing that.**

# LIFE APPLICATION

**Decorated Kids**

Have kids set their chairs in a circle, with one chair in the center. Have the person whose birthday is closest to Christmas sit in the center chair. Encourage kids to name talents and abilities they recognize and appreciate in the person who's in the center.

Besides the more obvious talents, encourage kids to recognize things such as friendliness, helpful attitudes and cheerfulness.

As kids list things, write them down with a marker on individual self-stick notes. Then have kids help you "decorate" the person in the center with the self-stick notes.

Give everyone a chance to be decorated, including you! Then ask:

● **How did it feel to get decorated?** (Really good; silly.)

● **How did it feel to tell others what you admire about them?** (That felt good, too; it was neat to see how it made them happy.)

# COMMITMENT

**Decoration Celebration**

Say: **It makes me feel good to look around at all you talented kids. I think God must be pleased, too. After all, he made all of you and gave you all these talents in the first place.**

Have kids find partners. Match older kids with younger ones as much as possible. Give kids each a photocopy of the "Decoration Celebration" handout (p. 45) and a pencil. Have partners help each other remove their self-stick notes and put them in the appropriate place on the handout.

Say: **Now, for each one of your self-stick notes, write or draw one way you can use that talent or ability for God's service.**

Ask older kids to help younger ones with this part of the activity. Older kids may be able to suggest things to draw based on the talent or ability. Encourage kids to share their "Decoration Celebration" handouts with their parents later.

# CLOSING

**Praising Partners**

Bring everyone together for a pair-share. Have partners each share how their partner plans to serve the Lord. Have older partners give their younger partners a little help if necessary. Throw a little confetti on each person as his or her partner shares.

Close with a prayer, thanking God for the talented kids in

43

the group and asking that God will help them serve faithfully and joyfully.

Then explain you're giving the class their first opportunity to serve the Lord joyfully by helping you pick up the confetti!

# DECORATION CELEBRATION!

Dear Lord, thanks for all these talents people recognize in me:

(Put your self-stick notes here.)

Here's how I want to use them for you:

"Serve the Lord with joy; come before him with singing" Psalm 100:2.

# My Feelings

# Feeling Good About Myself

## LESSON AIM

To help kids appreciate they're unique individuals created in God's image.

## OBJECTIVES

Kids will:
- identify what makes them feel good and bad;
- talk about God's love for them;
- celebrate each other's unique characteristics; and
- brainstorm ways to serve God.

## BIBLE BASIS

**Genesis 1:26-31a**

The creation of humankind is the crowning work of God's creation. Just before Adam's creation we see a unique conference between the members of the Trinity: "Let us make human beings in our image and likeness." All people carry within them some stamp of the divine—the ability to reason, to feel emotion and become morally responsible. Six times during the Creation story, God looked at his work and

## YOU'LL NEED

- ❑ balloons
- ❑ markers
- ❑ large garbage bag
- ❑ 9×12-inch pieces of posterboard with a small slit cut in the middle of each
- ❑ Bibles
- ❑ photocopies of the "God's Workmanship" handout (p. 56)
- ❑ scissors
- ❑ glue
- ❑ newspapers and magazines

49

pronounced it good. After the creation of humankind, he pronounced it very good.

As teachers, we have the unique opportunity to nurture the spiritual side of children while they are spiritually open and sensitive. We can help them discover the "homing" tendency that draws them to a relationship with the God in whose image they're made.

**Ephesians 2:10**

God has a purpose "planned in advance" for those who choose to follow him. No one needs to feel worthless or substandard. We are God's own works of art in process!

# UNDERSTANDING YOUR KIDS

It's not surprising that kids tend to value themselves as society values them. Those who are physically attractive, athletic, academically talented or socially adept tend to feel good about themselves because they find a great deal of acceptance from others. Kids need to see the values in God's family are different. Individuals are valued as God's unique creations, no matter what the outside package looks like.

Younger kids tend to compare their abilities to others'. Those who finish last, who are the most shy or who are the last to be picked for teams will often internalize these negative messages. "I'll never be good enough" can become a dangerous, negative mind-set very early in life.

Older kids find security through moving in flocks and through dressing, talking and acting like everyone else in their group. They need to be challenged to express their God-given individuality in creative and constructive ways.

**Balloon People**

As kids arrive, give them each a blown-up balloon and a marker. Place a large garbage bag at the front of the room.

Say: **I want you to draw a portrait of yourself on your balloon. Don't let anyone else see what you're drawing. When you finish your portrait, raise your hand and I'll come and put your balloon in my garbage bag. Then we're going to try to guess which balloon belongs to which person.**

After you've gathered all the balloon-portraits, pull them from the bag one by one and have people guess who they belong to. Once kids guess whose balloon it is, give it to that person, along with a piece of posterboard. Have kids each write their name on the posterboard and then push the tied-off end of their balloon through the slit in the center of the posterboard so the balloon will stand up on its own.

Ask:

● **How did it feel trying to draw your portrait on your balloon?** (It was hard; it made me think about what I'm really like.)

● **What helped you tell which balloon belonged to which person?** (The way they drew; the way it looked.)

● **What other things besides our appearance make us each different from everyone else?** (The things we like and don't like; the things we're good at.)

● **What's good about being the only person exactly like you on the whole earth?** (It makes me feel special.)

Have everyone stand in a circle holding their balloons. Then have kids each turn and face outward, take a step

> ### TEACHER TIP
>
> Younger kids who are just learning to write and draw may need some assistance holding their balloons as they draw on them.

51

forward and set down their balloon.

Have kids find partners. Be sure to have older kids pair up with younger ones who are just learning to write and spell.

Say: **I want each pair to visit all the balloons in the circle. On each posterboard, write one thing about that person that makes him or her unique and special.**

When all the pairs have visited all the balloons, have kids return to their own balloons to see what others wrote about them.

Then ask:

● **How did it feel writing nice things about all your classmates?** (It gave me a good feeling; it was hard.)

● **How did it feel seeing what other people think is special about you?** (I was surprised; it makes me feel warm inside.)

● **Were you surprised about some of the things people wrote about you? Why or why not?** (No, this was what I expected; yes, I didn't know people felt this way about me.)

Then say: **Today we're going to see what the Bible says about us as people and discover some reasons to feel good about ourselves.**

# BIBLE STUDY

**Ups and Downs (Genesis 1:26-31a)**

Have kids place their balloons along one wall of the room and then open their Bibles to Genesis 1:26-31a. Choose a narrator and three good readers to read in unison the parts spoken by God. Have these four kids stand facing the rest of the class.

Before the reading, have the rest of the class suggest ways the class could act out being trees, fish, birds, livestock and creatures that crawl along the ground. Explain to the class that on your cue, they are to imitate the trees or creatures the passage tells about. Then do the reading together.

After the narrator reads the final words, "it was very good," have everyone take a bow and sit down.

Ask:

● **What does it mean when the verse says everything God made was very good?** (God was pleased with all parts of creation.)

● **Does "very good" refer to you and me, too? Why or why not?** (Yes, we're a part of what God has made; no,

52

that was only the stuff God created then.)

● **How does it make you feel to know God says he made you and you are very good?** (It makes me feel very good; I'm surprised.)

● **Do you always feel good about yourself? Why or why not?** (No, sometimes I feel good about myself and sometimes I feel bad; yes, I'm good.)

Say: **Let's talk about what makes us feel good about ourselves and what makes us feel bad. I want everyone to stand in front of a chair. I'm going to read several statements out loud. If what I read would make you feel good about yourself, stand up on your chair. If it would make you feel bad, crouch down on the floor in front of your chair. If it would make you feel so-so, stay right where you are, standing in front of your chair.**

Read the following statements, pausing after each for kids' responses:

● **Your hair is messy and dirty.**

● **You drew a really neat picture, and it was put in the school art show.**

● **You broke a glass in the kitchen.**

● **Your parents grounded you for two days for having a messy room.**

● **You had a fight with your brother or sister.**

● **You got a new outfit, and you feel really cool in it.**

● **You got a letter from a friend you met at camp last summer.**

● **You started learning a musical instrument.**

● **You were the first to be picked when teams were chosen.**

● **You had to come to church with a black eye.**

Have kids sit down, and then ask:

● **Did we all feel good and bad about the same things?** (Mostly, but not exactly.)

● **What does that say about us?** (We're all different; we feel the same way about things.)

● **From the list I read, which would make you feel absolutely the worst?** Allow several kids to answer.

● **Pretend that thing happened; would that make you any less important to God or make him love you any less? Why or why not?** (No, God loves me no matter what; yes, he might be mad at me.)

Say: **A lot of what makes us feel good or bad is what happens on the outside—what kind of day we're having or how we look. But God cares about who we are on the inside. He loves us because he made us, and he made us in his image.**

53

## TEACHER TIP

Younger kids have a tendency to squeeze out enough glue to hold the entire church building together. Glue sticks are a better option for sticking paper to paper.

## TEACHER TIP

The younger kids in your class may not be able to read the words yet, but you'll be surprised how quickly they learn to "read" the verse after they've heard it a couple of times.

## TEACHER TIP

Keep kids on track during this activity by visiting each group to give encouragement and affirmation. Begin by checking on the youngest children first and then progressing to the oldest.

Ask:
● **What is God like?** (Great; loving; kind; just; creative.)
Say: **We are created in God's image. So we can be many of those things, too. God knows what we can be. And he wants us to become our very best for him.**

# LIFE APPLICATION

**God's Good Work**

Give kids each a photocopy of the "God's Workmanship" handout (p. 56), a pair of scissors and glue.

Have children return to the pairs they formed in the Balloon People activity. Point out the stack of newspapers and magazines.

Say: **I want you to work together in pairs to find the letters of your first name. Don't take more than one letter from any one place—be creative and find as many different kinds of letters as you can. Then glue the letters onto your handout to make your name.**

When all the names are complete, have kids read the verse aloud together.

Say: **Just as you carefully found and put together the letters of your name, God carefully put together each one of you. You are his workmanship—and we know what God makes is "very good."**

Ask:
● **What kinds of "good works" do you think this verse is talking about?** (It means helping people in need; telling others about Jesus; using our talents to serve God.)

# COMMITMENT

**Special People**

Say: **We've discovered several reasons to feel good about ourselves.**

Ask:
● **Who can tell me what they are?** (God made each of us unique; God made us "very good"; he made us to do good things.)

Have kids get their balloons and form groups of about four.

Say: **Look at the things kids wrote about the people in your group. Then tell what kinds of good works each**

54

**person could do for God.**

Kids might suggest things like helping parents, being kind to brothers and sisters, being honest or being friendly to other kids.

After three or four minutes, bring everyone together.

Say: **It's exciting to think about all the possibilities in this room. You're very special, not only because of what you can do, but also because of who you are.**

# CLOSING

### Thanking Our Creator

Form a circle. Have kids pile all the balloons in the center of the circle. Join hands and pray: **Dear Lord, thank you for each unique person in this class. Help them each to know that on their "up" days and on their "down" days you love and care for them. In Jesus' name, amen.**

Encourage kids to take their balloons and their "God's Workmanship" handouts home and talk them over with their parents.

Glue cut-out letters below to make your first name.

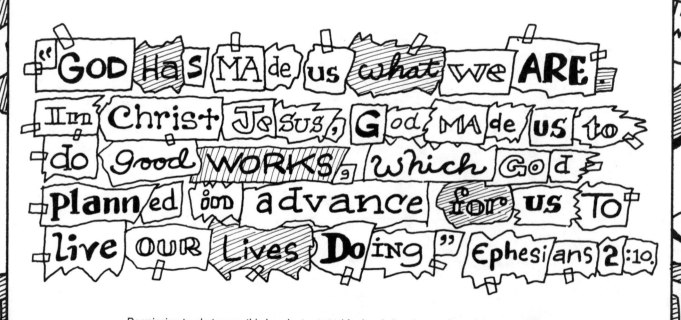

"GOD Has MAde us what we ARE In Christ Jesus, God MAde us to do good WORKS, which God Plann/ed in advance for us TO live OUR Lives Doing." Ephesians 2:10.

# Fears and Tears

**6**

To help kids learn God's comforting presence can be with them through scary and sad situations.

## OBJECTIVES

Kids will:
- play a game involving safety zones;
- learn how Jesus took care of the disciples' fears;
- identify times when they're afraid; and
- trust God to help them deal with their fears.

## BIBLE BASIS

**Matthew 8:23-27**

The Sea of Galilee was notorious for its sudden storms. The disciples, though some of them were experienced fishermen who had literally spent a lifetime on that body of water, were terrified when their little craft began to toss helplessly on the crashing waves in the middle of the night. They were amazed—and frustrated—that Jesus lay calmly sleeping in the front of the boat. Wasn't he aware of their peril? Didn't he care?

Jesus used the opportunity to demonstrate he is truly master of the wind and the waves. Jesus is master of the storms that buffet our lives, as well. Sometimes we may be tempted to wonder, as the disciples did, if he knows what's happening in our lives or if he cares. What we learn from this story is

## YOU'LL NEED

- ❏ masking tape or rope
- ❏ a roll of pennies
- ❏ a cuddly stuffed animal
- ❏ photocopies of the "Jesus Is My Safety Zone" handout (p. 64)
- ❏ pencils

## NOTE

This lesson works well with an intergenerational class. You may wish to invite whole families to join you for this session.

Jesus may not always make the storms disappear immediately, but he will walk with us through them.

**Matthew 28:20**

Jesus is the friend who sticks closer than a brother. Though kids may legitimately long for the reassuring physical presence of a trusted adult, Jesus' promise to be with those who trust in him is powerful indeed.

# UNDERSTANDING YOUR KIDS

"What's there to be afraid of?" I can remember my father asking that question when I was just a wee tot and the night-frights kept me from falling asleep. What's there to be afraid of? Plenty! Shadowy corners, familiar objects that loomed huge and strange in the dark, unknown things under the bed and behind the closet door, and the something that might pop up to get you if you got up to go to the bathroom. You may smile at that list, but children's fears are very real to them, and wise adults will take those fears seriously.

Kids of this generation have a lot more to handle than that standard list of fears. One of kids' biggest anxieties is being separated from parents. Divorce rates give credibility to that fear. On top of that, the television imports all kinds of fears right into living rooms—everything from war to psychopathic killers.

Now more than ever, kids of all ages need the assurance that God can be a personal, comforting, protecting presence in their lives.

# The Lesson ATTENTION GRABBER

**Safety Zone**

Set up the play area for this game by establishing four corners and a center circle as safety zones. Mark off the center circle with masking tape or rope; make it large enough so everyone can stand in it comfortably. Mark off a small triangle at each corner. Kids who are inside the circle and the corner triangles will be safe. Choose one person to be "It."

If you have adults in your class today, have them form the safety zones. Assign one adult to each corner and have the rest outline the center circle.

Say: **You can score a point and win a penny each time you run from the circle to one of the corners and back to the circle without being tagged. The circle and the corners are safety zones—you can't be tagged there. But only one person at a time can be in each corner. If you get tagged, you're frozen until another player tags you to unfreeze you.**

Stand in the center circle to hand out pennies as players score. Also be prepared to act as referee to determine whether or not kids make it to the safety zones before they're tagged.

Have a new person be "It" each time five people have scored.

Stop the game before interest lags. Bring kids together and help them focus on what you're about to say by leading them in some deep breaths.

Ask:

● **How did it feel to leave the safety zone?** (Scary; exciting.)

● **How did it feel to score and win a penny?** (It felt good; I wanted to win more.)

● **Which did you want to do more—stay safe or score? Explain.** (I wanted to score; I was afraid to try, I just wanted to stay safe.)

● **This game had safety zones where nothing bad could happen to you; do you have safety zones in real life? What are they?** (Home and church are my safety zones; my safety zone is when I'm with my parents or good friends because I know they won't let anything bad happen to me.)

● **How does it feel to go outside those safety zones?** (Really scary; it doesn't really bother me; I like to be out on my own.)

● **What happens to make people leave their safety zones even if they don't want to?** (Sometimes people have to move to a new place; sometimes parents divorce and we lose part of our safety zone; accidents and sickness sometimes pull us away from our safety zones.)

Say: **It's wonderful to have places where we feel safe and people who we feel safe with. But we can't always stay in our safety zones. And even in our safety zones**

# TEACHER TIP

Adjust the rules of this game to work for your group. You can make the boundaries of the game as large or as small as space permits. If too many people succeed in getting to the corners and back, let two or three people be "It." To even the odds for younger kids, let three of them be "It" at the same time.

scary things can sometimes happen. That's when it's nice to know Jesus is at our side.

# BIBLE STUDY

**Calming the Storm (Matthew 8:23-27)**

Say: **Today we're going to listen to a really scary story about what happened to Jesus' disciples. And you're going to help me tell it.**

Practice each of these cues and responses with the class:

● **Whenever I say "boat," everyone say "creeeak" and pretend you're pulling hard on the oars.**

● **Whenever I say "disciples," all the boys (and men) count to 12 really fast.**

● **Whenever I say "wind," the girls (and women) cup their hands around their mouths and blow.**

● **Whenever I say "waves," put your hands side by side and make waves in front of you.**

● **Whenever I say "Jesus," point to upward and say, "Christ, the Lord."**

As you tell the Jesus Calms the Sea story on page 61, be sure to put an emphasis on each of the underlined words; then pause for kids to respond.

Say: **Here we go! Everybody stick together so you don't get too scared.**

Read the story. After you finish, have kids give themselves a round of applause for helping you tell the story. Then ask:

● **What happened that made the disciples feel unsafe?** (Their boat got in a bad storm; they were afraid of drowning.)

● **What did they do to get help?** (They woke Jesus up.)

● **What did Jesus do to make things okay again?** (He told the wind and the waves to be still.)

● **How could he do that?** (He's God's son—he can do anything.)

● **Can Jesus help us the way he helped the disciples in the storm? Why or why not?** (Yes, Jesus can still do anything; no, he doesn't work that way now.)

● **Can Jesus help us even though we can't see him or touch him? Why or why not?** (Yes, he's always with us; no, sometimes we don't ask him.)

---

## TEACHER TIP

Rehearse the cues in scrambled order several times before you begin reading Jesus Calms the Sea.

# Jesus Calms the Sea

The disciples were just exhausted. All day crowds and crowds of people had been following Jesus, listening as he taught and watching as he healed the sick. Now the sun was beginning to set over the Sea of Galilee. Seeing how tired his disciples were, Jesus said, "Let's get in a boat and go over to the other side of the lake." It would be good for all of them to get away from the crowds for a while.

The disciples rowed away from the shore while Jesus went to the front of the boat and lay down on a cushion. The waves lapped gently against the side of the boat, lulling Jesus into a peaceful sleep. But suddenly a wind began to blow dark clouds across the sky. The waves weren't so gentle anymore. The little boat began to pitch and rock. The disciples began to get a little worried. But Jesus still lay sleeping in the front of the boat.

Then the wind grew stronger still. The spray from the waves got the disciples all wet. This was getting to be a bad storm! But Jesus still lay sleeping in the front of the boat.

By the time the fishing boat reached the center of the lake, the wind had turned into a angry gale that whipped the waves so high they washed right over the boat. The disciples were terrified. They thought they might drown. But Jesus still lay sleeping in the front of the boat.

Finally, someone went and shook Jesus. "Master," he cried, "don't you care if we drown?" Jesus looked around. He listened to the howling wind. He felt the cold, stinging spray as waves crashed over the little boat. He saw the fear in the faces of his disciples. Then Jesus stood, stretched out his arms to the wind and the waves, and commanded: "Peace! Be still!"

And all at once the wind died down and the waves became completely calm. Then he asked the disciples: "Why are you so afraid? Where is your faith?"

Jesus showed his power over the wind and the waves that day on the Sea of Galilee. Just as he cared for his disciples in that little storm-tossed boat, he will care for you.

## TEACHER TIP

If you have a very large inter-generational class, you may wish to form two or three groups. Encourage people in each group to share how God helped them through scary situations.

# LIFE APPLICATION

**Someone to Hang On To**

Ask:

● **Can anybody tell how Jesus helped you in a scary situation?** Give kids a chance to share. It would be helpful to share a story from your own experience at this point. If you have other adults in the class, they might also tell about times when God helped them face a scary situation.

After several people have shared, bring out a cuddly stuffed animal, preferably one that's clean but well-worn. Pass it around the class and have everyone hug it. In a larger class pass two or three stuffed animals at once.

Ask:

● **Why does everybody like to have stuffed animals around?** (They're cute; they feel good to hang on to; they never get mad.)

● **What does it feel like to hug an animal like this?** (It feels warm; cuddly; good.)

● **Do you ever hug a stuffed animal when you're scared or sad?** (Sometimes.)

● **How is the feeling you get from hugging a stuffed animal like how it feels to trust Jesus when you're scared or sad?** (Jesus comforts me; when I ask for his help, I remember he loves me.)

● **How is trusting Jesus different from hugging a stuffed animal?** (Jesus is really alive and has power to help me.)

# COMMITMENT

**Facing Our Fears**

Say: **Just before Jesus went back to heaven, he made a promise to his followers. Let's look at that promise.**

Give each person a photocopy of the "Jesus Is My Safety Zone" handout (p. 64) and a pencil. Point out the Bible verse at the bottom of the handout.

Say: **This is the promise I'm talking about. Let's read it aloud together.**

Say: **This is what I really want you to remember from today's class. Jesus promises he will always be with us. And having Jesus with us is even better than having a teddy bear or an older brother, or even parents,**

## TEACHER TIP

Younger children will be able to "read" the verse after the class repeats it a couple of times.

**because Jesus is the Son of God, and he has power to help us!**

Have kids (and adults) use the space on the handout to draw or write about a scary situation they sometimes face. Allow two or three minutes for drawing and writing, and then ask volunteers each to tell about the scary situations they put on their handout. Kids may be surprised to learn adults have fears, too, and even though they're grown up, they also trust in Jesus to help them in scary situations.

Ask:

● **How does it feel to see Jesus with his arms around you in your scary situation?** (It feels good.)

Say: **The next time you're afraid, I hope you'll remember Jesus will be with you.**

# CLOSING

**Always There**

Gather everyone in the Safety Zone circle. If you have adults in the class, have them make an outer circle with the kids inside.

Close with a prayer similar to this one: **Jesus, thank you for being our safety zone. Help us to remember the next time we're really scared that you are with us. Amen.**

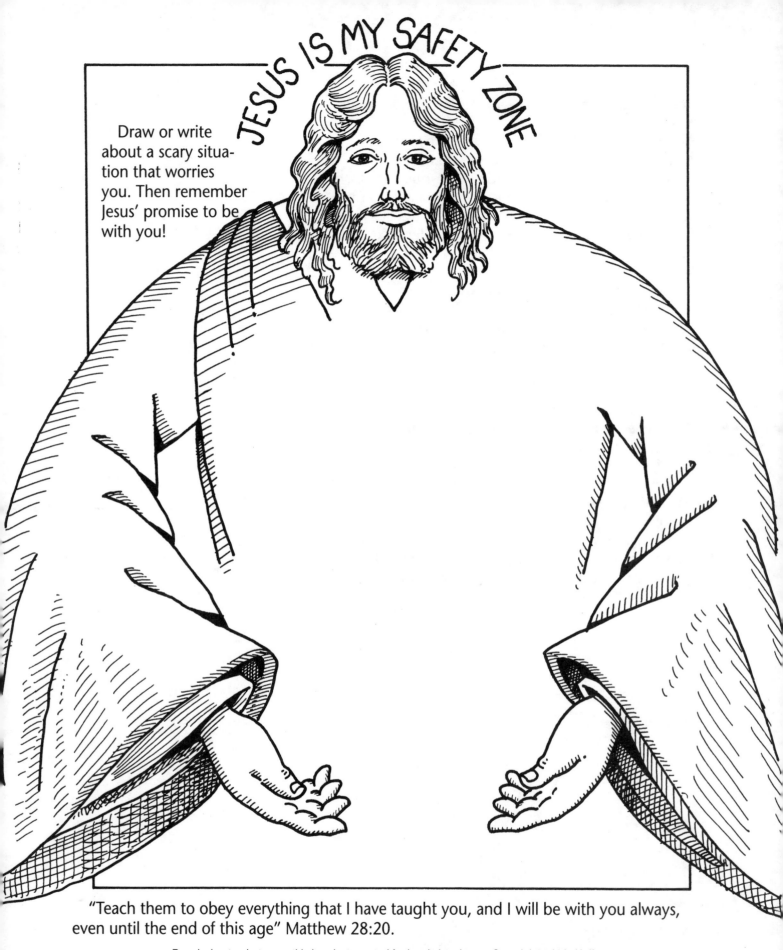

JESUS IS MY SAFETY ZONE

Draw or write about a scary situation that worries you. Then remember Jesus' promise to be with you!

"Teach them to obey everything that I have taught you, and I will be with you always, even until the end of this age" Matthew 28:20.

# Temptation: The Great Escape

## LESSON AIM

To help kids realize the importance of avoiding temptation.

## OBJECTIVES

Kids will:
- play a game that simulates the excitement of temptation;
- learn what happened to a Bible character who dabbled in forbidden things;
- develop strategies for resisting temptation; and
- be reminded of the importance of their relationship with God.

## YOU'LL NEED

- ❑ a bandana
- ❑ one marble for each student
- ❑ a table
- ❑ Bibles
- ❑ newsprint
- ❑ marker
- ❑ tape
- ❑ photocopies of the "Walk Away!" handout (p. 71)
- ❑ pencils

## BIBLE BASIS

**Joshua 6:1—7:26**

Fascination with dabbling in forbidden territory goes as far back as Adam and Eve. God's rules were clear. Choosing to ignore those rules even "just this once" changed all of humanity's relationship with God forever.

To God, the clearing of Canaan was serious business. All inhabitants of the towns and countryside were to be killed, right down to the livestock. All valuables were to be brought to the treasury of the Tabernacle. God wanted his people to be untainted by anything associated with pagan Canaanite religions.

But when an Israelite named Achan caught sight of a beautiful Babylonian robe and a pile of gold and silver, he thought, "Surely it wouldn't matter if I took this stuff just this once..." Direct disobedience brought serious consequences: a lost battle, and public disgrace and the stoning of Achan's entire family.

God's rules are for real today, just as they were in Achan's time. There's only one thing to do in the face of temptation: Walk away!

### 1 Corinthians 10:13

Kids tend to think the problems and temptations they face are different from what anybody else faces. But Paul assures us God doesn't allow temptations that millions of others haven't faced, too. And besides that, kids can gain confidence that no temptation is too great to overcome. God promises a way out—and he'll be there to help if we let him.

## UNDERSTANDING YOUR KIDS

Kids know all about temptation. It starts with the forbidden dip into the cookie jar and eventually grows to potentially life-threatening proportions as kids are offered drugs and alcohol. It's important for us as adults to see what lies behind kids' desires to overstep safe, established boundaries.

For both younger and older kids the motivation is often curiosity—the desire to know things firsthand rather than accepting the knowledge and warnings of those in authority. Rebellion also plays a part. Kids want to set their own boundaries rather than accept the limitations others set.

In today's "whatever works for you" society, kids need God's boundaries more than ever. They need to understand God isn't some mean old man in the sky; he gave us rules because he loves us. And kids need to see a few moments of excitement dabbling in forbidden zones can bring disastrous results.

# The Lesson

**Steal the Jewels**

If it's a bright, sunny day, play this game outside on a grassy surface. Have kids stand in a circle about 10 feet across. Choose one person to be "It." Tie up the marbles in a bandana and put these "jewels" at the feet of whoever's "It." If you have more than 20 kids, form multiple circles. You'll need a bandana and marbles for each circle.

Say: **The object of this game is to steal the jewels. But be careful—if the person who's "It" touches you, you're frozen until the end of the game. If you manage to steal the jewels and get back to your place in the circle, then you get to be "It" and a new game starts.**

You can play several rounds of this game because someone usually gets the jewels in just a few seconds. This game works really well with kids of mixed ages because younger kids can dart in and out quickly, and they have the advantage of being smaller targets.

After a few rounds of play, ask:

● **How did it feel to steal the jewels?** (Fun; exciting.)

● **How did it feel going after the jewels, knowing you might get frozen?** (It was exciting and scary; there was the chance I could get the jewels without getting caught.)

● **How are those feelings like when you're tempted to do something wrong that you know is wrong?** (I really want to do it, but I'm afraid I might get caught.)

● **How is playing this game like giving in to temptation?** (We go after the jewels even though we know it's dangerous.)

● **How is it different?** (It's just a game—we don't really break any rules or do anything wrong; we're supposed to go after the jewels.)

Say: **Temptation usually involves breaking rules. Or doing something we know we're not supposed to do. Usually there's something we want; we know what the rules are, and we make a choice. The person we're going to learn about in today's Bible story made a bad choice. Let's see what happened to him.**

## TEACHER TIP

If kids have trouble stealing the jewels, hint that they can all go for the bandana at once. Most of the kids will get frozen, but someone is bound to get through.

# BIBLE STUDY

**Tempted! (Joshua 6:1—7:26)**

Say: **After more than 300 years of slavery in Egypt and 40 years of camping in the desert, the Hebrew people are ready for a new home in the land of Canaan. There's just one little problem. There are already people in the land, and they're not about to move out so God's people can move in. This means war!**

The people of Canaan lived in cities with high, strong walls. We're going to make one of those cities right now.

Have kids help you put a table in the center of the room. Put the jewels (still in the bandana) from the Steal the Jewels activity under the center of the table. Then form two groups, with older kids in one group and younger kids in the other. Have the older kids form a city wall by standing around the table in a circle, facing outward.

Say: **We've just built the city of Jericho. Now the rest of you are going to be the army that conquers the city.**

Ask:

● **Can anyone tell me how God told Joshua to attack Jericho?** Several kids may be familiar with the directions Joshua gave to his army. Review them by having volunteers read aloud Joshua 6:1-8, 14-16.

Say to the younger kids: **Okay, you soldiers have your marching orders. Let's march around Jericho seven times.**

Lead the soldiers in a vigorous march seven times around the "walls." Then lead the soldiers in a shout on the count of three, and cue the walls to collapse.

Have everyone sit on the floor as you continue the story.

Say: **That was a pretty impressive victory! But a problem came up when one of the soldiers didn't follow orders. Joshua told his troops to bring all the treasure out of the city and give it to the priests as an offering to God. So they did—all except for one man named Achan. Achan came up to a house and looked inside.**

Lead kids in peeking under the table.

Say: **There he found treasure—bags of silver and gold and a beautiful robe.**

Open the bandana and display the marbles that represent the treasure.

Ask:

● **What was Achan supposed to do with the treasure?** (Bring it to the priests.)

Say: **But he thought: "I could be rich! The priests would never miss this little bit of gold and silver." So he took the treasure and hid it in his tent.**

**So Achan became a rich man and lived happily ever after. Right? Wrong! Because Achan gave in to temptation, terrible things happened. The Hebrews lost their next battle, and God showed Joshua that Achan was to blame. So to remove the sin from the Hebrew people, Achan and his whole family were killed.**

Ask:

● **Why did this story have such a sad ending?** (Because Achan gave in to temptation.)

● **How do you think Achan felt after he got caught?** (Guilty; scared; sad.)

● **Do you think Achan would have felt that way even if he hadn't been caught? Why or why not?** (Yes, he still would've felt guilty and scared because he knew he had done something wrong; no, he made a choice to disobey God, so he didn't care what God or anybody else thought.)

Say: **God doesn't usually deal with disobedience today by killing people. But when we disobey him, we're hurting our friendship with him. And it makes him sad.**

# LIFE APPLICATION

**Temptation Today**

Ask:

● **Do you think people are ever glad about giving in to temptation, even if they don't get caught? Why or why not?** (Yes, some people don't care about sin; no, people who don't get caught still feel sad and guilty.)

● **What kinds of things tempt kids today?** (Cheating in school; using bad language; talking back to parents and teachers; trying cigarettes or alcohol; watching the wrong kinds of TV shows and movies; taking candy or tapes from stores.) List kids' answers down one side of a sheet of newsprint taped to a wall.

● **What happens when kids give in to temptations like these?** For every temptation on the list, have kids suggest a consequence. Jot their answers on the other half of the newsprint.

# COMMITMENT

**Walking Away**

Give kids each a photocopy of the "Walk Away!" handout (p. 71) and a pencil. Have a volunteer read the Bible verse out loud.

Say: **God wants us to walk away from things that tempt us. Let's look at the list we made of things that tempt us. How could we walk away from them?**

Read the items from the list, and have kids tell ways to walk away from each one. Then have kids use the blank space on the handout to draw something that tempts them. Demonstrate how to fold the handout so the tempting thing "disappears."

After kids have finished drawing, ask:

● **How does walking away from temptation make it disappear?** (The temptation doesn't really disappear, but walking away helps me avoid giving in.)

● **How does thinking about temptation make it harder to resist?** (The more I think about something, the more I want it.)

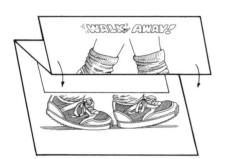

# CLOSING

**The Greatest Treasure**

Give kids each one of the marbles from the Steal the Jewels activity.

Say: **Things that tempt us may look good for a while. But there are always consequences to pay if we give in. Take this marble with you today to help you remember God is our greatest treasure, and we don't want to give in to any temptations and destroy our relationship with him.**

Close with prayer, asking God to help kids walk away from temptations that come into their lives.

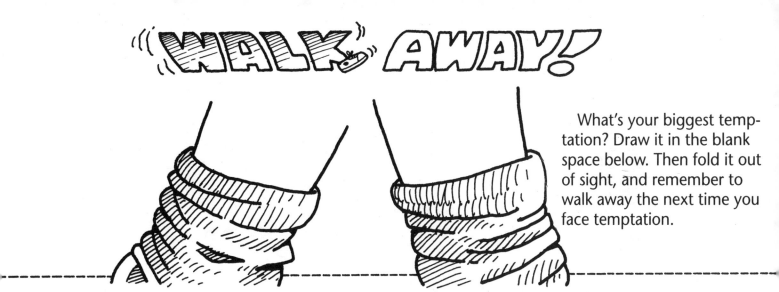

# WALK AWAY!

What's your biggest temptation? Draw it in the blank space below. Then fold it out of sight, and remember to walk away the next time you face temptation.

"The only temptation that has come to you is that which everyone has. But you can trust God, who will not permit you to be tempted more than you can stand. But when you are tempted, he will also give you a way to escape so that you will be able to stand it" 1 Corinthians 10:13.

# When Life's Not Fair

## LESSON AIM

To help kids trust that God is in control even when life seems unfair.

## OBJECTIVES

Kids will:
● discuss reactions to an unfair situation;
● discover how God worked to protect his people in an unfair situation; and
● commit to trusting God when they can't understand or see the outcome.

## BIBLE BASIS

**Esther 1:9—8:12**

Talk about spies and international intrigue! The book of Esther contains one of the most exciting stories in the Bible. A wicked prime minister plots the downfall of the Jews, but God comes to the rescue in response to the pleas of a beautiful, obedient queen and her people.

We, in our simple human wisdom, would like to predict God would always bring down the bad guys and rescue the faithful, as happens in the book of Esther. But God's ways are higher than ours, and there are times when he allows the righteous to suffer. The bottom line for this lesson is things don't always turn out "fair," but we can trust God to care for us and work out his plans in the end.

## YOU'LL NEED

❏ small prizes
❏ a blindfold
❏ Bibles
❏ photocopies of the "Mystery Mosaic" handout (p. 79)
❏ crayons

**Psalm 37:1-3**

Our society teaches the outcome is everything. The end justifies the means. This psalm directly contradicts that modern philosophy. Our task is simply to trust in the Lord and do good. We can, and should, leave the results with him.

# UNDERSTANDING YOUR KIDS

Kids have a tremendously strong sense of justice. Everybody should get the same number of cookies. If I'm nice to you, you should be nice to me. Kids who play fair should win. If we're caught fighting, my punishment should be no worse than yours.

Younger kids trust parents, teachers and other authority figures to legislate fairness in their lives. And they get very upset when justice as they see it isn't done.

Usually by third or fourth grade kids have figured out that life isn't always going to be fair. Parents divorce. Cheaters and bullies sometimes carry the day. Pets and loved ones get sick and die. And trying hard doesn't always mean succeeding. When these things happen, kids can begin to feel that life is out of control.

Kids (and adults!) need to see God is working, even in the midst of devastating circumstances, and his justice will prevail in the end.

# The Lesson

## ATTENTION GRABBER

**Overpowered**

Say: **We're going to begin today with some arm-wrestling contests. I'll pair you up for the first match. The winners will each receive one of these.**

Show what you brought for prizes.

As you pair kids up, make sure one person in each pair is obviously larger and stronger than the other, so that the outcome of the match will be obvious.

73

**TEACHER TIP**

As you set up these obviously unfair contests, kids may protest. Be very positive and encouraging. Say, "I know, but let's just hang in there and see what happens."

Say "go" and have kids start their matches. Ask all the winners to stand up, and give them each a prize. By now, most of the kids will be objecting and saying, "That's not fair!"

Ask:

● **How did you feel about these arm-wrestling matches?** (They weren't fair!)

● **What was unfair about the way I set things up?** (Some people were a lot stronger than their partners; some kids didn't have a chance.)

● **How did it feel to have to arm-wrestle someone when you knew you would lose? when you knew you would win?** (I didn't even want to try; I felt sorry for the other person.)

● **How were these contests like unfair things that sometimes happen in real life?** (Sometimes teachers or parents make decisions that aren't fair; sometimes all the good guys get on one team at school and we know we'll lose.)

● **What's the most unfair thing that ever happened to you?** (I got blamed for something I didn't do at school; I got sick the day we were supposed to go to Disney World; my parents got a divorce.)

● **How do you feel when unfair things happen?** (Angry; like I want God to fix it.)

Say: **Today we're going to participate in a Bible story that started out with a really unfair situation. Things were so bad, it looked like God's people might be wiped out completely. Let's see what happened.**

## BIBLE STUDY

**An Evil Plot (Esther 1:9—8:12)**

Practice each of these cues and responses with the class:

● **Whenever I say "Esther," the girls fan their hands around their faces and say "ah!"**

● **Whenever I say "king," the boys say, "May he live forever!"**

● **Whenever I say "Mordecai," press your hands together and say, "A devout Jew."**

● **Whenever I say "Haman," everyone boo and hiss.**

● **Whenever I say "Lord," respond by saying "God Almighty!"**

Then say: **Ready? Here we go with the story, The Queen and the Evil Plot.**

**TEACHER TIP**

Practice the cues and responses several times in random order before you begin the story. If you have mostly younger children, you may wish to use only three or four cues and responses.

74

Read aloud The Queen and the Evil Plot story on pages 76-77. Pause after each underlined word to let kids do their actions.

Ask:

● **How would you have felt if you had been one of the Jews who was going to be killed?** (Angry; scared.)

● **Instead of getting angry or frustrated at God, what did Mordecai and Esther do?** (They fasted, and got other people to fast with them; they trusted God to help them; they came up with a wise plan.)

● **How do you think God wants us to respond when unfair things happen in our lives?** (He wants us to pray and trust him; to act wisely.)

# LIFE APPLICATION

**Why Worry?**

Say: **God wants us to trust him when we face scary situations—just like Esther and Mordecai did. Let's see what that kind of trust feels like.**

If you have more than 15 kids, you may want to do this activity in groups of 10 kids to save time. Have kids form pairs. Pair older kids with younger ones. Send one pair out of the room. Have the other pairs form an obstacle course with their bodies. They can sit, stand, kneel or create arches.

Blindfold one member of the pair who left the room. Then have the sighted partner lead the blindfolded partner around the obstacle course. Have the partners change roles and go through the course again.

Send another pair out of the room and have the rest of the kids create a different obstacle course. Continue in this manner until each person has gone through the obstacle course blindfolded.

Then gather kids in a circle and ask:

● **How did it feel going through the obstacle course without being able to see?** (It was scary; it was kind of fun; I didn't want to do it.)

● **How important was your partner's help?** (Really important; I'd never make it without a partner.)

● **How did it feel to trust your partner?** (I didn't know if I could trust him; I wish she had talked to me more.)

● **How is that like trusting God when we don't know how things are going to turn out in our lives?** (We know God is there, but we don't know exactly what he's doing;

# The Queen and the Evil Plot

A mighty king ruled the land of Persia. And a lovely young Jewish girl, Esther, had recently become his queen. One day Mordecai Esther's Uncle Mordecai worked at the palace. One day Mordecai overheard two men plotting to kill the king. He told Queen Esther, who told the king, and the plot was stopped.

Shortly after that, an evil man named Haman became prime minister. He was second in command in the whole kingdom. Haman became so powerful everyone bowed when he walked by—everyone but Mordecai, that is. Haman hated Mordecai because he wouldn't bow down. So Haman thought up an evil plan to get rid of him.

Haman persuaded the king that the Jews were rebellious and dangerous. So the king gave Haman permission to issue a royal decree. On a particular day, all the Jews in Persia were to be killed. And whoever killed them could keep all their money and property. How horrible! How unfair!

When Mordecai heard about this evil plot, he told Queen Esther. "You must go plead with the king, or our people will be destroyed," he said.

The queen was frightened. She could be killed for entering the royal throne room without permission. So Queen Esther told Mordecai, "Gather all the Jews in the city to fast for three days. Don't eat anything!"

Three days later Queen Esther put on her royal robes and entered the throne room. The king welcomed her—she was safe. The Lord had answered the people's prayers. The queen invited the king and Haman to a special banquet that evening. At the banquet, the king asked: "What is your request? Tell me, and I will grant it." But the queen only smiled and invited the two men to another banquet the next evening.

Haman was proud to be honored at a special banquet given by the queen. And he looked forward to getting rid of Mordecai, the one person who would not bow to him. "Why not get rid of that pesky Jew right away?" his wife suggested. "You can ask permission in the morning to hang him and then go on your way to the queen's banquet." Haman liked the idea, and he immediately had a tall gallows built for hanging Mordecai.

But the Lord had different plans. That night the king couldn't sleep. So he had his servants read to him from the records of the kingdom. They read about the time Mordecai had saved the king's life. "I must honor this man," the king said.

The next morning, Haman arrived to ask permission to hang Mordecai. But before he could speak, the king asked him, "What should I do to honor a man who truly pleases me?"

Haman thought the honor would be for himself. "Oh, Sire, I would put royal robes on him and have someone lead him through the streets on your own horse, shouting, 'This is the way the king honors those who truly please him!' " "Excellent!" the king replied. "Go find Mordecai and do for him just what you've described."

Haman couldn't believe his ears, but he obeyed and led Mordecai through the streets of the city in royal splendor. Then he hurried to the queen's banquet.

"Tell us why you've invited us here," said the king. "What is your wish? I will grant it, even if it is half my kingdom!"

Queen Esther replied, "Please, Your Majesty, save my life and the lives of my people. There is an evil plot against us!"

"Who would dare harm you?" the king demanded.

"He would!" replied Queen Esther, pointing at Haman who had turned pale with fright.

One of the servants came forward and said: "Your Majesty, this man has just had a tall gallows built. He was planning to hang Mordecai on it—the very same man who saved your life!"

"Hang Haman on his own gallows!" the king ordered. And so they did.

Soon afterward, Mordecai became the new prime minister. He got permission to issue a royal decree telling the Jews to defend themselves on the day they were to be killed. The Lord didn't let his people down. Instead of being destroyed, they became stronger than ever.

sometimes we wish we could really see God and have him explain things to us.)

Have kids open their Bibles to Psalm 37:1-3, and have a volunteer read the passage aloud.

Ask:

● **What things doesn't God want us to do?** (Worry; be jealous.)

● **What does God want us to do?** (Trust him to work things out.)

● **What's hard about trusting God when life seems unfair?** (Sometimes it seems like he's not helping us or he doesn't care.)

● **How is trusting God like trusting your partner? How is it different? Explain.** (I have to rely on him when I don't understand what's going on; God won't ever mess up or let me down, but my partner might.)

# COMMITMENT

### Just Trust

Give kids each a photocopy of the "Mystery Mosaic" handout (p. 79) and a crayon.

Say: **When you solve this mystery, you'll know exactly what God wants you to do the next time you feel like life isn't fair.**

Allow time for kids to color in the spaces with the dots and discover the words "just trust." Encourage kids to keep the secret until everyone has discovered the words. Have older kids help younger kids figure the words out.

Then have kids each use the framed space to draw or write about one unfair situation in their life (or in the world) in which they need to trust God.

# CLOSING

### God at Work

Bring everyone together and ask volunteers to share what they drew or wrote about. Join hands and close with prayer, asking God to work out things for the best in each of these situations, just as he did for Mordecai and Queen Esther.

# My Relationships
# With Others

# Telling the Truth

## LESSON AIM

To help kids realize God expects honesty from his people.

## OBJECTIVES

Kids will:
- participate in creating a silly story;
- explore a scriptural example of honesty;
- role play telling the truth in difficult situations; and
- ask God for help in being honest.

## BIBLE BASIS

**2 Chronicles 18:3-34**

This story happens during the period of the divided kingdom. Jehoshaphat, king of Judah, was a godly man. But Ahab, king of Israel, made a habit of defying and mocking God. Ahab kept a flock of false prophets around him. Their main purpose in life was keeping the king happy. Micaiah, the one prophet who was in touch with God, had gained himself a poor reputation with Ahab because he insisted on telling the truth. In this story, Micaiah tells the truth even when he knows the king will throw him in prison.

In our society, people often do and say "whatever works," rather than whatever is honest. Our challenge is to be as honest, in touch with God and willing to take a stand as Micaiah was.

## YOU'LL NEED

- ❏ pen
- ❏ two crowns
- ❏ three bathrobes or bed sheets
- ❏ false beards and wigs
- ❏ Bibles
- ❏ photocopies of the skit "To War or Not to War?" (p. 87)
- ❏ a long piece of rope or clothesline
- ❏ a photocopy of the "Tell the Truth" handout (p. 90)
- ❏ scissors

## NOTE

This lesson works well with an intergenerational class. You may wish to invite whole families to join you for this session.

**John 8:31-32**

When Jesus says, "The truth will make you free," he's talking primarily about the freedom that comes from a relationship with God. Once we're free from sin, we're also free to tell the truth, under any and all circumstances.

# UNDERSTANDING YOUR KIDS

Even kids from wonderful Christian homes seem to learn to lie just about as soon as they learn to talk. There is something deceitful in human nature that causes us to want to cover our tracks. Honest living is an ongoing challenge for all Christians, kids and adults alike. The key thing to teach kids is God will forgive us for wrongdoing if we're honest about it. Any temporary reprieve gained by dishonest behavior will quickly pass; the loss of integrity is a far greater consequence to pay in the end.

Younger kids can learn that it's okay to tell the truth—if their honest confessions of faults and errors are met with forgiveness and a chance to make a fresh start.

Older kids have mastered the half-truth or "white lie." They need to see that God calls us to perfect integrity and that it's better to live with the consequences of telling the truth than with a murky conscience.

# The Lesson ATTENTION GRABBER

**Sunday Sillies**

Say: **You've heard of the Sunday funnies in the newspaper. Today in class we're going to start out with the Sunday Sillies.**

Have kids form three groups. Take turns asking the three groups for the words you need to fill in the story Sunday Sillies on page 86. Make sure you have an adult or an older child in each group who will be able to help the others come up with the right kinds of words for the story.

Say: **I'll ask your groups to give me different kinds of words or names. When it's your group's turn, make a huddle and then call out the word you decide on. When we've filled in all the blanks, I'll read you our Sunday Sillies.** Jot kids' words down in the blanks of the Sunday Sillies story, and then read the story, inserting the kids' words as you read.

After you've read the completed story to the class, ask:

● **What's so funny about this story?** (The words don't really fit; it sounds weird.)

● **What do we call it when we make up things that aren't true?** (Lying.)

● **How is the Sunday Sillies like lying?** (We're just making it up as we go along; it's not really true.)

● **How is it different from lying?** (We followed your instructions; we're not doing it to be dishonest.)

● **How is copying someone else's paper like lying?** (We're pretending to know something we don't really know.)

● **When are most people tempted to lie?** (To keep out of trouble.)

Say: **It's fun to make up stories. But in real life, God wants us to tell the truth—even when it's hard. Today we're going to learn about a man in the Bible who did just that.**

# BIBLE STUDY

**Truth or Consequences (2 Chronicles 18:3-34)**

Explain that today's Bible study is in the form of a skit, and everyone gets to take part. If you've invited adults for an intergenerational class, ask three men to take the parts of Ahab, Jehoshaphat and Micaiah. Have students take the parts of the narrator and the messenger. Tell the rest of the class to say "ooo!" when you point at them.

Have your characters put on the costume items you brought—crowns, bathrobes or bed sheets, beards and wigs.

You may choose to read the narrative directly from the Bible, signaling characters to read as their lines come up. Or use photocopies of To War or Not to War? on page 87, a version of the story in skit format.

After the skit, have everyone give the characters a round of applause.

# Sunday Sillies

_____ didn't like _____. In fact, it was her most
(girl's name)                (subject in school)

_____ subject. So, she never studied or even did her _____.
(adjective)                                                      (thing)

At the end of the quarter, she was getting a very bad _____.
                                                            (thing)

"Oh no," she _____. "I'll get a really _____ grade in this
              (past tense of verb)                (adjective)

subject. What am I going to _____?"
                              (verb)

On the day of the final test, she was feeling _____. Suddenly she
                                                 (adjective)

had a/an _____ idea. _____ was sitting right beside her.
          (adjective)       (boy's name)

He was a/an _____ student. She could see his paper _____.
             (adjective)                                   (adverb)

"I'll _____ his paper," she thought. "Then I'll be sure to get a
       (verb)

_____ grade.
(adjective)

Suddenly the teacher's shadow _____ across her desk. The
                                (past tense of verb)

teacher snatched up the test paper and _____ into the
                                        (past tense of verb)

_____. _____ knew she was in big _____.
(thing)      (same girl's name)                (thing)

# To War or Not to War?

**NARRATOR:** We're about to witness a meeting between two great kings. (Signal kids to "ooo!") Jehoshaphat is the king of Judah. He's a good man who tries his best to follow God. Ahab is the king of Israel. He's a wicked man who does what he pleases and ignores God's laws.

**AHAB:** Jehoshaphat, great to see you, ol' buddy ol' pal. Doesn't this look like great weather for a war? What d'ya say we get our armies together and go attack Ramoth in Gilead? We could wipe it out in no time and add a few juicy items to our royal treasuries. How about it?

**JEHOSHAPHAT:** Well sure, I always like to help out a neighbor. But don't you think we ought to check with God about this? I mean, war is serious stuff.

**AHAB:** Okay, okay. I figured you'd say something like that. (Shouts) Call the prophets together!

**NARRATOR:** Suddenly, 400 prophets appeared on the scene. (Signal kids to "ooo!") "Go to war!" they all shouted. "God will give you success." But Jehoshaphat wasn't convinced.

**JEHOSHAPHAT:** Uh, not to be rude, but don't you have any real prophets?

**AHAB:** I was afraid you'd ask that. Yes, we have a real prophet. His name is Micaiah. But he always prophesies bad things for me. I can't stand the guy! (Signal kids to "ooo!")

**JEHOSHAPHAT:** You really shouldn't talk that way about the Lord's prophet.

**AHAB:** Yeah, yeah, I know. Okay, somebody go get Mr. Bad News.

**NARRATOR:** The king sent a messenger to get Micaiah.

**MESSENGER:** Look, Micaiah, there are 400 other prophets there, and they're all saying, "Go to war." Give yourself a break! Go along with them and tell the king what he wants to hear.

**MICAIAH:** I can only say what God tells me to say.

**MESSENGER:** This could get nasty. (Signal kids to "ooo!")

**AHAB:** Oh, there you are, Micaiah. Nice of you to drop in. Well, what's the word? Should we go to war or not?

**MICAIAH:** (Insincerely) Sure, go ahead. You're bound to win.

**AHAB:** (Storming) Quit clowning around. What are you really thinking?

**MICAIAH:** (Looking upward) I see your armies scattered across the hillside. Their leader is dead. (Signal kids to "ooo!")

**AHAB:** I knew it. Didn't I tell you he never says anything good about me?

**NARRATOR:** Micaiah's truthful prophecy made the other prophets so mad, one of them came and slapped Micaiah in the face. (Signal kids to "ooo!") And Ahab was so mad, he slapped Micaiah in prison and gave him only bread and water. (Signal kids to "ooo!")

**AHAB:** Forget Mr. Bad News. Let's go to war anyway.

**NARRATOR:** So Ahab and Jehoshaphat and their armies attacked. Just to play it safe, Ahab dressed like a common soldier. But an arrow went right between the sections of his armor, and the wicked king of Israel died that very day. (Signal kids to "ooo!")

Ask:

● **Do you think it was easy for Micaiah to tell the truth? Why or why not?** (No, he knew he could get in trouble with the king; yes, he knew God would protect him.)

● **Why did Micaiah choose to tell the truth when so many people were against him and he knew he would get in trouble?** (He wanted to obey God; he knew God would be on his side no matter what happened.)

● **Have you ever been in a situation where it took a lot of courage to tell the truth? Explain.** Answers will vary. If you have adults in the class, children will be especially excited to hear about struggles their parents or grandparents had in telling the truth when they were younger.

# LIFE APPLICATION

**Made Free**

Hold up the rope or clothesline. Have everyone stand in a circle.

Say: **I want each of you to think about one time you were not perfectly honest. You don't have to say it out loud—just think about it. Then wrap the rope around yourself one time and pass it on to the next person.**

Coach the wrapping process so that everyone ends up wound snugly, but not too tightly, together.

Make sure you're the last person to wrap up. Then ask:

● **How does it feel to be all wrapped up like this?** (Trapped; scary.)

● **How is this like what happens when we tell a lie?** (Sooner or later we'll get caught; we get trapped in a web of lies to cover up the first one.)

● **What can set us free?** (God's forgiveness sets us free.)

Say: **Jesus told his disciples: "If you continue to obey my teaching, you are truly my followers. Then you will know the truth, and the truth will make you free." Jesus wants us to accept the forgiveness he offers and then live honestly before God and before men.**

**If you've never asked forgiveness for a dishonest act, this would be a good time to do it. Then, as you unwind yourselves, say Jesus' words, "The truth will make you free."**

---

## TEACHER TIP

If your group is larger than 15, you may wish to bring two ropes and do this activity in two separate groups.

---

# COMMITMENT

**To Tell the Truth**

After everyone has unwound themselves, say:

**Jesus wants to set us free from dishonesty and lies. Let's practice telling the truth by role playing some difficult truth-telling situations.**

Form four groups. Give each group one of the role-plays from the "Tell the Truth" handout (p. 90). Give groups a few minutes to plan their role-plays. Then have them take turns performing.

After each role-play, ask why it was best to tell the truth in that situation. Encourage kids to tell what might happen if the character tried to hide what really happened.

(p. 90)

---

**TEACHER TIP**

Encourage groups to be creative in "casting" their role-plays. Younger kids can take the parent roles; adults can play young children.

# CLOSING

**Prayer for Courage**

Close with prayer, asking God for the courage to be honest even when it's difficult.

As kids leave, have them shake hands with and say to six people, "The truth will make you free."

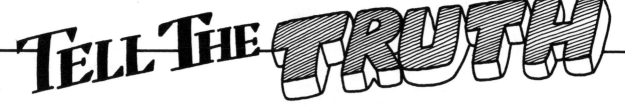

Photocopy and cut apart these truth-telling situations.

---

Jesus expects us to be honest, even when it's hard. Role play ways to tell the truth in this situation.

### A Piece of Cake

There was one piece of cake left. It was supposed to be your brother's. But you were really hungry, and you ate it. Now your brother is screaming that his cake is gone.

---

Jesus expects us to be honest, even when it's hard. Role play ways to tell the truth in this situation.

### An Important Message

Your dad was expecting an important call from his boss. You were supposed to stay home and take the message. You forgot and went out to play catch with your friends. You remember just as your dad is pulling into the driveway.

---

Jesus expects us to be honest, even when it's hard. Role play ways to tell the truth in this situation.

### An Artful Answer

Your friend wants to enter a picture in an art show. He asks you what you think of it. You think you've seen him draw other pictures that are a lot better.

---

Jesus expects us to be honest, even when it's hard. Role play ways to tell the truth in this situation.

### The Stain

You're having a fight with your sister when your mom isn't home. You get really mad and throw a pillow at her. The pillow knocks her glass of red Kool-Aid onto the carpet. Your mom comes home and finds the stain.

# Caring for God's World

**10**

## LESSON AIM

To help kids accept responsibility for caring for God's Earth.

## OBJECTIVES

Kids will:
- play games to celebrate creation and simulate pollution;
- discover God's instructions about caring for the Earth;
- evaluate ways people contribute to pollution; and
- plan ways to keep the Earth clean and safe for living.

## BIBLE BASIS

**Genesis 2:15-20**

"The Lord God put the man in the garden of Eden to care for it and work it." This verse gives a solid foundation for both a work ethic and ecology, all in one sentence. God didn't leave Adam to wander aimlessly through the garden—he gave Adam a purpose for living. Work and responsibility for our living space are not the result of human sin, but part of God's original plan for people.

God made humans the rulers and caretakers of his newly

## YOU'LL NEED

- ❏ one blindfold for every two kids or items collected from nature placed in individual lunch bags
- ❏ Bible
- ❏ newspapers
- ❏ paper grocery bags
- ❏ newsprint
- ❏ markers
- ❏ photocopies of the "God's Wonderful World" handout (p. 98)
- ❏ crayons

91

created world. It's a sacred trust that all believers share, not only for practical reasons, but theological ones, as well.

**Psalm 104:24**

The great variety displayed in the natural world is a fitting tribute to the creativity of the creator! After spending a day in nature, even the most determined agnostic must wonder how all this beauty could possibly have happened by chance.

# UNDERSTANDING YOUR KIDS

This is one of many lessons in which the teachers might very well learn something from the students. Kids are constantly hearing anti-pollution messages at school as well as from mass media. Some of those messages are coming from questionable sources and promote an incorrect worship of nature. We need to help kids sort through the good, biblically sound messages and the not-so-positive New Age ones.

But it's a good thing kids are learning to "think green," because they're the ones who will have to live with or repair the damage done by preceding generations. Christian kids have even more reason to get involved in environmental matters. It's their God-given task!

Being excited about taking care of the environment and living out that concern on a day-to-day basis are two different matters. When you're out and about, it's a lot easier to pitch an aluminum can than to carry it home to recycle it. Real conservation means remembering to turn off lights, hiking or biking instead of hitching a car ride, and cooling off in the shade instead of in the air conditioning. Kids are often tempted to do things the easy way instead of the "green" way. They need lots of encouragement and affirmation to develop and stick to an environment-conscious lifestyle that will keep God's Earth green for future generations.

### Hug-a-Tree

Tell the class you're going to begin this lesson with a very different kind of nature study. Have kids form pairs—preferably with an older and younger student in each pair. Take the group outside and walk to a place where there are several trees.

Gather everyone in the middle of the trees and say: **One partner will put on a blindfold. The other partner will lead the blindfolded partner to a tree, any tree. When you get to your tree, give it a hug and then feel it very carefully with your hands. Try to learn everything about that tree you can without looking at it. Then your partner will lead you back to the center, spin you around three times and take off the blindfold.**

After everyone has hugged a tree, been spun around and sat down, remove the blindfolds and find out how many kids can identify the trees they hugged. If it's a nice day, sit down on the grass to discuss the experience.

Ask:

● **How did it feel to hug a tree?** (I felt silly; it felt kind of neat.)

● **How did you feel when you recognized the tree you hugged?** (I was glad; I was surprised I could recognize it.)

● **What do you like about trees?** (They give us shade and fruit; they're pretty to look at.)

Say: **Trees are a wonderful part of God's creation. They're part of God's gift to us, and we need to take care of them. God put trees in the garden where he made the very first man and woman. Today, we're going to talk about what happened in that garden and about the important job God gave to that first man.**

### Creation Mysteries

Collect several items from nature that have different textures and place them in separate brown lunch bags. You might include a smooth leaf, flower petals, a thistle, a pine branch, garden soil, a bird feather, a rock and a piece of animal fur. Have kids take turns feeling what's in each bag without looking. After everyone has had a chance to touch the

## TEACHER TIP

If it's not possible to take your kids outside or if your area doesn't have many trees, use the Creation Mysteries Attention-Grabber below.

mystery items, let the younger kids tell you what they think each bag contains. Then spread out the mystery items on a table.

Ask:

● **What can you learn about things without using your eyes?** (What they feel like; how they're put together.)

● **Which was your favorite thing to touch?** Answers will differ.

Say: **Did you know God gave us the very important job of taking care of all these things? It happened way back when God created the world. Let's find out about it by taking a trip back to the beginning of the Earth.**

# BIBLE STUDY

**The World God Made (Genesis 2:15-20)**

Say: **Today we're going to make a copy of the Garden of Eden—where God put the first people he ever made.**

Have kids volunteer for the following parts by raising their hands. Explain that kids will stay in their seats now and then play their roles when you read through the Bible passage.

● **First of all, our garden has a man named Adam. Who wants to be Adam?**

● **The Bible talks about a river running through the garden. We need two or three people to stretch out on the ground to make the river.**

● **Now we need a couple of trees. Who wants to be a tree?**

● **Now we need two more trees—the tree of life and the tree of having knowledge of good and evil.**

● **Last of all, we need people to be all kinds of birds and animals.**

Be sure all kids who haven't been chosen for another part become birds and animals.

Say: **Great! Now we're all ready. Listen for your part and be ready to take your place in the garden as I read the story from the Bible.**

Read Genesis 2:15-20 aloud, pausing to cue kids to perform their assigned parts. Some students may be excited about this kind of Bible study and want to do it again. That's fine—do it again if you have time.

Ask:

● **What do you think the Garden of Eden was like?** (It was full of beautiful trees and flowers and friendly animals.)

## TEACHER TIP

You may want to have an older student read the Bible passage so you can be free to coach the children on when to take their places and how to play their parts.

94

● **What job did God give Adam?** (Adam was supposed to work in the garden and take care of it; he gave names to all the animals.)

● **Has anyone here ever helped take care of a garden? What do you like about it?** (Yes, it's fun to dig in the dirt and smell the flowers; I like to eat the vegetables.)

Say: **I think Adam enjoyed living in the garden, taking care of it and watching over all the animals. But soon Adam and Eve sinned, and God made them leave the garden. Then more and more people were born, and they began to spread all over the Earth. Now we have the whole world to take care of.**

Ask:

● **Do you think we're doing a very good job? Why or why not?** Kids' responses may differ.

# LIFE APPLICATION

**Clean Sweep**

Say: **Let's see what kind of job we're doing taking care of the part of God's world we live in. We're going to go outside for a "look and listen" walk. I want you to be totally silent—no talking at all. Listen for all the sounds you can hear, and look around for any garbage or pollution you can see. Don't talk until we're sitting here in our places again.**

Take the kids for a two-minute walk. Then bring them back inside and discuss what they saw and heard. Ask about the natural sounds and the human-made sounds. Talk about natural beauty and human-made pollution. If you want, have kids go back outside and pick up any trash they saw on the walk.

Ask:

● **How do you think God feels when he sees how people have messed up the beautiful world he created?** (Sad; angry; disgusted.)

Say: **Let's play a game called Clean Sweep and see if that will help us understand.**

Have kids count off by threes. Have groups 1 and 2 form a big circle together. Give each child in the circle a sheet of newspaper. Give kids in group 3 each a paper grocery bag, and have them get on their hands and knees in the middle of the circle.

Say: **When I say "go," groups 1 and 2 will start tear-**

ing their newspapers into little pieces and throwing the pieces into the circle. Group 3 will try to keep the circle clean by picking up all the paper shreds and putting them in their bags. I'll call time after one minute, and then we'll see if group 3 was able to keep the circle clean. Ready? Go!

After the minute is up, have everyone help the kids in group 3 gather the paper shreds. Then ask:

● **How did it feel to throw all that garbage into the circle? Explain.** (It was fun, but I felt bad about making the other group work so hard.)

● **How did it feel trying to keep the circle clean? Explain.** (It was discouraging; it was hard work because there were more people messing it up than helping clean it up.)

● **How is this game like what's happening in the real world?** (A lot of people are polluting and only a few are trying to clean it up.)

● **Do you think God feels kind of like the kids in group 3 felt? Why or why not?** (Yes, he gave people this beautiful world to live in, but they keep messing it up; no, he doesn't get mad.)

● **Does being a Christian make a difference in the way we feel about keeping the Earth clean? Why or why not?** (Yes, God gave us the job of caring for the Earth; no, I'm not picking up someone else's trash.)

Say: **Tell me about the things you do to help care for the Earth. List kids' responses on newsprint.**

Ask:

● **What else can we do to help care for the Earth?** If kids haven't already mentioned these things, bring them up: we can recycle, walk or ride a bike instead of asking for a ride in a car, correctly take care of our trash, use water and other resources carefully.

Record these ideas on newsprint, as well.

# COMMITMENT

**Our Favorite Things**

Give kids each a photocopy of the "God's Wonderful World" handout (p. 98) and a crayon. Point out the Bible verse at the bottom and ask a volunteer to read it aloud.

Say: **You can see this handout is divided in half. On the left side of the page, draw your favorite thing from**

---

## TEACHER TIP

If you have extra time, have kids return to their three groups and create posters or banners urging people to take good care of the wonderful world God has given us.

creation—it can be a flower, a tree, an animal or even a mountain. On the right side, draw or write about one thing you'll do this week to help take care of God's wonderful world.

Allow a few minutes for drawing and writing, and then ask volunteers to share what they drew or wrote about. Encourage kids to share their plans with their parents.

# CLOSING

**For All the Earth**

Gather kids in a circle and lead them in sentence prayers. Have volunteers finish the sentence, "Thank you, God, for creating ..." Close the prayer time by asking God's help in taking good care of his wonderful world.

# GOD'S WONDERFUL WORLD!

Draw your favorite thing in all of God's creation.

Draw or write about one thing you'll do this week to help care for God's world.

"Lord, you have made many things; with your wisdom you made them all. The earth is full of your riches" Psalm 104:24.

# God Talk, Good Talk

## 11

## LESSON AIM

To help kids realize the importance of being encouraging and positive in their speech.

## OBJECTIVES

Kids will:
- observe how putdowns deflate a "balloon person";
- listen to a Bible character tell how putdowns harmed his family;
- practice making encouraging comments; and
- prepare messages of encouragement for others.

## BIBLE BASIS

**Genesis 21:1-14**

God shows us in this very early story of a family's struggle and eventual breakdown how damaging mockery and putdowns can be. God had promised to make Abraham the father of many nations. But for scores of years Abraham wasn't able to become the father of even one child. Finally Sarah, Abraham's wife, urged Abraham to have a child with her servant Hagar. When Hagar became pregnant, she mocked Sarah, causing terrible heartache and discord in the household. Hagar eventually gave birth to Ishmael. But God told Abraham that Ishmael was not the son he had promised—Sarah would conceive in her old age and bear him a son.

## YOU'LL NEED

- ❏ round balloons
- ❏ long balloons
- ❏ masking tape
- ❏ string
- ❏ markers
- ❏ straight pins
- ❏ an adult to play the role of Abraham (optional)
- ❏ bathrobe for Abraham's costume
- ❏ Bible
- ❏ overalls and shirt on a hanger
- ❏ newspapers
- ❏ photocopies of the "Talking Card" handout (p. 106)
- ❏ scissors
- ❏ pencils

When Sarah gave birth to Isaac, Ishmael must have felt cast off and displaced, even though scripture says Abraham loved him. Ishmael's mockery of Isaac at a party given in Isaac's honor was the proverbial last straw. Sarah demanded—and got—immediate dismissal of Hagar and Ishmael from the family.

**Ephesians 4:29**

In this passage, Paul warns Christians against evil speaking, but then he goes on to state the same principle in a positive way: Say what encourages people and builds them up.

# UNDERSTANDING YOUR KIDS

"Where did you come up with that outfit?" That comment has stuck with me since sixth grade. I can remember exactly what I was wearing, who said it, who witnessed it, where we were standing in the school and what the weather was like!

To paraphrase a childish expression: Sticks and stones may break my bones, but bones heal in a few weeks. Putdowns will almost always hurt me and probably stick with me for years to come.

Putdowns are easy to understand. If my words cut someone down, then I'm suddenly bigger in comparison. Unfortunately, putdowns know no age limit. For kids at the lower end of your age-group a putdown may be something like, "Can't you even tie your shoes yet?" Older kids may come out with charming phrases like, "Don't be such a sleaze-ball."

The good news is putdowns and negative speech are habits—and habits can be changed. A positive spirit is as contagious as a negative one. This lesson gives you a chance to show kids it feels good to make others feel good—and it pleases God, as well.

### Hey, Mr. Balloon Man!

As kids arrive have them form groups of about five. Give each group one round balloon, four long balloons, tape, string and a marker. Explain that each group is to build a balloon person by blowing up the balloons and taping or tying them together. Groups can use the round balloon as the head and the four long balloons as arms and legs. Have kids use markers to give their balloon people faces.

Have groups bring their finished balloon people to the front. Say to one of the balloon people: I think you're full of hot air.

Follow the putdown with sticking a straight pin into one of the balloons. Give kids each a straight pin and invite kids to insult other groups' balloon people and to pop one balloon after each putdown.

After all the balloon people have been destroyed, ask:

● **How did it feel to see your balloon person being destroyed?** (It felt terrible; I wanted to protect him.)

● **How did it feel to insult other balloon people and pop the balloons? Explain.** (It was fun at first, but when I saw my balloon person getting hurt I wanted to stop.)

● **How is that like what happens when people put you down?** (It feels like they stuck me with a pin; it feels like I shrink and become an ugly little blob.)

● **Do you think putdowns really harm people? Why or why not?** (Yes, people may say they don't care, but deep inside they really do get hurt; no, words can't hurt me.)

Say: **We know putdowns cause hurt and angry feelings. Today we're going to see how putdowns tore apart a Bible-time family. As a matter of fact, the father of that family is going to pay us a visit and tell us the sad story—right now!**

# BIBLE STUDY

**A Sad Day (Genesis 21:1-14)**

Tell kids a very famous person from the Old Testament is going to visit your class. If you recruited an adult to play the part of Abraham, cue him to enter now.

Or you may choose to have one of your older boys play Abraham. Make sure you choose a good reader. Let the other kids use the bathrobe to dress him as a Bible-time character, and then welcome him to class with a round of applause. Have him read or recite the story A Visit From Abraham on page 103.

After Abraham makes his exit, ask:

● **Why was Abraham so sad?** (He had to send Ishmael away.)

● **Why did Ishmael get sent away?** (For making fun of Isaac.)

● **Why do you think Ishmael acted that way?** (He was jealous of all the attention Isaac was getting.)

● **When have you felt jealous like Ishmael did?** Allow kids to respond.

● **What happens when we make fun of others?** (Their feelings get hurt; we get in trouble; they may try to get back at us by putting us down.)

● **Is it ever smart or right to put other people down? Why or why not?** (No, it hurts people; yes, sometimes people deserve it.)

Say: **Sometimes it feels good just for a minute when we put someone down. But the good feeling never lasts. And we usually end up paying for it in the end, just as Ishmael did. Let's see what the Bible has to say about putdowns.**

# LIFE APPLICATION

**Stuffed With Affirmations**

Have a volunteer read Ephesians 4:29 aloud. Bring out your overalls and shirt and a stack of newspapers. Hang the hanger with the clothes on a nail or over a door.

Say: **We saw how putdowns destroyed our balloon people. Now we're going to do just the opposite. We're going to build this person up by giving encouragement and saying things that make a person feel good.**

# A Visit From Abraham

Hello, children. It's nice to see all of you here today. I've always loved children. But for a long time I didn't think I'd have any of my own. You see, I was even older than your grandparents when my first son was born. Since my wife Sarah had been unable to have children, I had a son with my wife's servant Hagar. That was a common practice back in our day.

I was so proud of young Ishmael. He was a fine lad. But poor Sarah, my wife, longed for a son of her own. We prayed for years that God would send us a son. And it finally happened when Sarah was over 90 years old! We were so happy when our son was born we named him Isaac, which means laughter.

But things didn't stay happy around our house for too long. Ishmael was used to being the only son, and he was jealous of Isaac. He teased Isaac and mocked him all the time. And every time it happened, Isaac would run to his mother and complain. Then Sarah would come to me and say: "I've had it with Ishmael. He's always putting Isaac down. One day he'll go too far."

And that's exactly what happened. One day we were having a big birthday party for Isaac. Ishmael hung around the tent, picking at Isaac and making fun of him all day. Finally Sarah blew up. "That's it!" she shouted. "I want Hagar and her son out of here today. Ishmael has made fun of Isaac for the last time. I want them out of here *now!*"

It was awful. I loved both my sons. But I could see Sarah was right. Ishmael would just keep making trouble as long as he was around. So early the next morning I packed up some food and water and sent Hagar and Ishmael away.

I cried as I watched them go, but I knew God would take care of them. If only Ishmael could have learned to treat Isaac nicer, this could have been different . . .

(Abraham wanders away sadly shaking his head.)

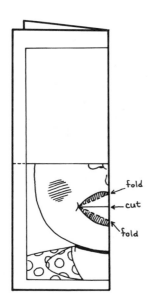

**Fold in half lengthwise and cut horizontal slit in the mouth.**

**Open and fold in quarters with mouth on inside.**

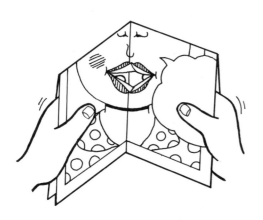

**Push lips out from center fold.**

Wad up a piece of newspaper, stuff it into the shirt and say: **I'm glad you came to class today.**

Let kids take turns stuffing the figure with newspapers and saying one encouraging comment with each newspaper wad they stuff. Guide the process so the arms, legs and body each get some stuffing.

When the figure is well-stuffed, say: **Look at how the encouraging things we said have built up this person. Let's see if this works in real life.**

Have kids take turns standing in front of the class. Give the rest of the children 20 seconds to make positive comments about the person who's standing. After everyone—including you!—has received encouragement and affirmation, ask:

● **How did it feel to hear everyone's encouraging comments?** Allow students to share their feelings.

# COMMITMENT

**Encouraging Words**

Say: **We don't want all these encouraging words to stay here in our class. We want to encourage each other after class and during the week, too. We're going to make cards to give to people this week.**

Give kids each a photocopy of the "Talking Card" handout (p. 106), a pair of scissors and a pencil. Demonstrate how to fold and cut the card so the lips move.

Have kids form pairs, younger kids with older kids, to work on their cards. Have partners discuss who to send the card to and what message of encouragement to write in the speech balloon. Let older kids do the writing for younger ones whose writing skills aren't yet developed.

# CLOSING

**Boisterous Buildups**

Have kids stand in a circle holding their completed cards. Explain that on the count of three, kids will make their cards talk all at once, saying the encouraging message that's written on them.

Say: **That sounds terrific. Let's remember to use words that build people up, not put them down.**

Bring the stuffed-overall person into the center of the

circle. Close with a prayer similar to this one: **Dear Lord, thank you for the encouraging words we've all heard from each other today. Help us to keep building each other up. In Jesus' name, amen.**

Remind kids to show their talking cards to their parents and then to send the cards to the people they thought of when they wrote their encouraging messages.

# Talking Card

"When you talk, do not say harmful
things, but say what people need—
words that will help others become
stronger. Then what you say will do
good to those who listen to you."
Ephesians 4:29.

I just had to tell you . . .

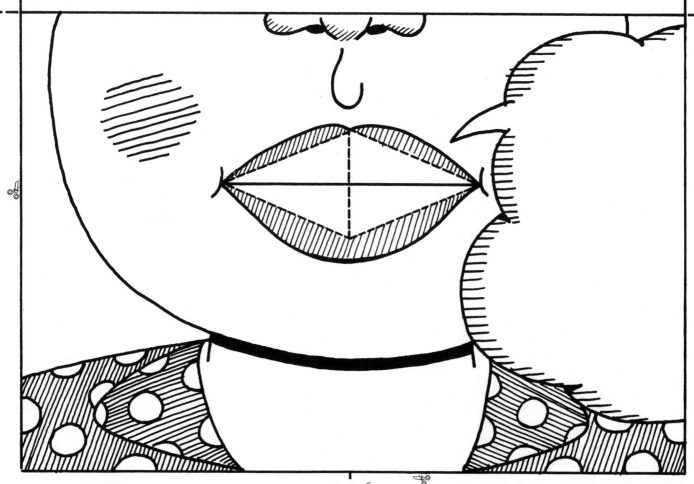

# Sharing What We Have

## 12

## LESSON AIM

To help kids discover joy in sharing what they have with others.

## OBJECTIVES

Kids will:
● discover how sharing can benefit everyone;
● learn how a woman in the Bible shared the last food she had;
● make an inventory of what they have to share; and
● identify three things they will share this week.

## BIBLE BASIS

**1 Kings 17:1-16**

This story is set against a time of great famine in the land of Israel. The prophet Elijah told King Ahab that God would not allow rain or dew until the king repented of his wicked ways. Then Elijah ran for his life!

Elijah eventually made his way to the home of a widow and asked for food. Widows had no rights and few defenders in Bible times. Asking a widow for food would be like asking a

## YOU'LL NEED

❑ a jar of peanut butter
❑ a jar of jelly
❑ a loaf of bread
❑ four knives
❑ paper plates
❑ napkins
❑ photocopies of the "Share Sheet" handout (p. 114p)
❑ markers
❑ masking tape
❑ Bibles

homeless person for a blanket. But the woman realized this was no ordinary person who asked. She recognized Elijah's request as God's will and willingly obeyed.

We can find joy in sharing even the things that are most precious to us when our sharing is done in obedience to God's will and in recognition that God, our provider, will not fail us.

### Philippians 4:19

This remarkable promise was not written by a wealthy person surrounded by all the comforts of life. It was written by Paul, probably while he was in prison or under house arrest in Rome. Paul's circumstances give special meaning to his faith that God would care for those who care for the needs of others.

# UNDERSTANDING YOUR KIDS

"Mine!" is one of the first words toddlers learn. "My" and "me" are quick to follow. Our healthy instincts for self-preservation carry over very naturally into "self-ishness." There are those few, rare children who seem to be naturally bighearted and generous. But most kids learn sharing by example and by receiving praise and attention for generous behavior.

Children share more readily as they get older and more mature. Some four- and five-year-olds may not want to share at all—they may be perfectly happy to take whatever interests them and to go play by themselves in a corner. Most kids are well into their elementary school years before they learn to share for the sheer joy of meeting a need or making another person happy.

## The Impossible Sandwich

As kids arrive direct them into four groups.

Say: **We're going to start off today with a treat.**

Give the first group a jar of peanut butter, the second group a jar of jelly, the third group a loaf of bread and the fourth group four knives. Give everyone paper plates and napkins.

Then say: **Go ahead and eat!**

Kids may or may not figure out that they can all enjoy peanut butter and jelly sandwiches if the groups all share what they have. The kids in the group with the peanut butter may just dig in with their fingers! If this happens, drop a little hint like, "I wonder what would happen if everyone shared ..."

When everyone is finally enjoying peanut butter and jelly sandwiches, ask the kids who received only jelly or knives:

● **How did you feel at the beginning when you only had a jar of jelly or a few knives?** (I didn't know what to do; I wished we'd gotten the peanut butter; I hoped the people who got the other stuff would share with us.)

Ask the kids who received the bread and peanut butter:

● **How did you feel about getting something you could eat right away when other kids didn't?** (I felt lucky; I felt sorry for the other kids; I wanted to share right away.)

● **How did you feel when everyone started sharing?** (I got excited; I felt a lot better.)

● **When is it hard to share things?** (When it seems like I have to do all the giving; when it's something I really want for myself.)

● **When is it easy to share?** (When there's plenty to go around; when it doesn't really feel like I'm giving up anything.)

Say: **Today you're going to help me tell a story from the Bible about a woman who shared, even when it was really hard.**

**A Little to Share (1 Kings 17:1-16)**
Practice each of these cues and responses with the class:

● **When I say "brook," everybody say "babble, babble" and make piano fingers, like water running in a stream.**

● **When I say "ravens," everybody flap your arms with your elbows out and say "caw, caw."**

● **When I say "Elijah," the boys point upward and say "the Tishbite."**

Take a moment to explain that Elijah was a famous prophet. He was called Elijah the Tishbite because he came from the town of Tishbeh.

● **When I say "widow," the girls pull their hands down over their faces like a veil.**

● **When I say "bread," everybody rub your tummies and say "yum, yum."**

Then say: **Ready? Here we go with the story Elijah and the Widow.**

Read aloud Elijah and the Widow on page 111. Pause after each underlined word to let kids do their actions.

After the story, ask:

● **Do you think it was easy or hard for the widow to share her bread with Elijah? Explain.** (It was hard, she barely had enough for herself and her son; it was easy, she had nothing to lose.)

● **If she only had a little food left, why did she share it?** (Elijah told her God wouldn't let her run out of oil until it rained again and people could grow more food.)

● **Why did she believe Elijah?** (She knew he was a prophet from God.)

Say: **The interesting thing about this story is God made sure the widow never ran out of oil and flour. So the bread she shared with Elijah wasn't really her own—it came from God.**

**God made a promise to take care of the widow when she shared her bread. God makes a promise like this to us, too, in the book of Philippians.**

---

## TEACHER TIP

If you have a very large group, you might choose one child to be the leader for each cue. The leaders could stand in front of the group and lead the responses each time their words come up in the story.

# Elijah and the Widow

Once there was a wicked king named Ahab. He was so wicked, God sent the prophet <u>Elijah</u> to talk to him. "There won't be any rain until you repent of your evil ways," <u>Elijah</u> told the king. This made the wicked King Ahab very angry. So God told <u>Elijah</u> to go hide by a <u>brook</u>. God said, "You can drink from the <u>brook</u>, and I will send <u>ravens</u> with <u>bread</u> for you."

So <u>Elijah</u> went to the <u>brook</u>. Every morning the <u>ravens</u> brought him <u>bread</u> and meat. And even though there was no rain and it was very dry in the whole country, <u>Elijah</u> could drink from the <u>brook</u>.

But finally the <u>brook</u> dried up. So God sent <u>Elijah</u> to the town of Zarephath where he found a kind <u>widow</u> gathering sticks for a fire. "Would you bring me some <u>bread</u>?" <u>Elijah</u> asked the <u>widow</u>. The <u>widow</u> answered, "I don't have any <u>bread</u>, just a little oil and flour, enough to make just one more meal for me and my son."

<u>Elijah</u> said, "Make me some <u>bread</u> first. God will not let you run out of oil and flour until it rains again. The <u>widow</u> did as <u>Elijah</u> said. She made <u>bread</u> for <u>Elijah</u> and herself and her son for many days. Just as God promised, the oil and flour never ran out. There was always enough to make more <u>bread</u>. God took care of <u>Elijah</u> and the kind <u>widow</u> who shared, and God can take care of you, too!

**Sharing Time**

Give kids each a photocopy of the "Share Sheet" handout (p. 114), a marker and a piece of masking tape. Have a volunteer read Philippians 4:19 aloud.

Say: **Another famous Bible person, the Apostle Paul, counted on people to share with him. Paul was arrested and put in jail for teaching people about Jesus. His friends in different churches shared food and clothes and money with him. And he told those people who shared with him that God would keep on taking care of their needs, just as God took care of the widow who shared with Elijah.**

Have someone read aloud Philippians 4:19 again.

Say: **This promise is for us, too, when we share what we have with people in need. The question is: What do we have to share? We're going to find out!**

Have kids find partners. Make sure your youngest students who are just learning to read and write are paired with older students who can help them. If you have more than 20 kids in your class, you may want to do this activity in two groups.

Say: **Write your own name on the blank line at the top of your Share Sheet. Then ask your partner to tape it to your back.**

Explain that each pair will get together with all the other pairs. Kids will take turns writing on each person's Share Sheet what they think that person has to share with others. Encourage kids to think about everything from hugs and friendly smiles to allowances and computer games.

Keep kids moving around the classroom two by two until each set of partners has written on the Share Sheets of all the other pairs.

Say: **Now it's time to see what other people think you have to share! Take off your partner's Share Sheet and hand it to him or her.**

Give kids a moment to look over what people wrote on their Share Sheets. Then ask:

● **How does it feel to see all the things you have to share?** (It's surprising; it makes me feel good.)

● **Look at all the things on your sheet; where do they come from?** (From parents; from inside of me; from God.)

Discuss the fact that everything comes from God in the end. Allowances may come from parents, but parents get their jobs and their abilities to work from God. If we have friendly

## TEACHER TIP

The job of writing on each other's back is easier if kids use markers, but make sure they are washable markers that won't bleed through the Share Sheets and stain kids' clothes. Crayons work well also.

smiles and hugs to share, it's because God put love for other people in our hearts.

Then say: **Maybe you're thinking of something you have to share that nobody wrote on your Share Sheet. Go ahead and write or draw it now.**

Give kids a moment to think and write or draw. Encourage older kids to help younger ones with ideas.

Say: **Now look over your whole list and decide if each thing on it would be easy or hard for you to share. Put a circle around the things that would be easy for you to share. Underline things that would be hard for you to share. Then tell your partner why you marked things the way you did.**

Allow a couple of minutes for kids to mark their lists and talk with their partners.

# COMMITMENT

### Choosing to Share

After two or three minutes, call time and say:

**Choose three things from your list you'd like to share with someone during the coming week. Draw a box around those things. Then tell your partner what you're going to share and who you're going to share each thing with.**

# CLOSING

### Our Sharing God

Bring everyone together and ask for a pair-share, where each person tells one thing his or her partner is going to share this week.

Then say: **The neat thing about sharing things God gives us is that we don't need to worry about running out. He promises in Philippians 4:19 to take care of our needs as we take care of the needs of others.**

Close with prayer, asking God to give kids a generous spirit and to help them follow through on the sharing they've planned for this week.

# SHARE SHEET

_____ has these things to share:

# Handling Anger and Conflict

**13**

## LESSON AIM

To help kids learn appropriate ways to express anger and handle conflict situations.

## OBJECTIVES

Kids will:
- discover how venting anger can hurt people;
- learn how a Bible character unselfishly settled a conflict;
- apply new techniques for settling conflicts; and
- make a commitment to express anger appropriately.

## BIBLE BASIS

**Genesis 13:1-18**

Abraham and Lot had traveled together from Egypt and were preparing to set up more permanent residence in Canaan. As the patriarch, Abraham had every right to tell Lot where to go and when to leave. Instead, he chose to avoid conflict and allowed Lot to take the fertile land in the valley. What a contrast to the "fight for your rights" mentality we see so often in today's society!

Abraham was able to surrender his rights because he

## YOU'LL NEED

- ❏ a can of soft drink
- ❏ newsprint
- ❏ markers
- ❏ masking tape
- ❏ two bags of large marshmallows
- ❏ photocopies of the "Peacemaker Certificate" handout (p. 122)
- ❏ pencils

trusted God completely. God honored that trust by promising Abraham the whole land and a nation of descendants to fill it.

### Ephesians 4:2-3

Humility, gentleness, patience and love are not always the easiest qualities to demonstrate, especially when a person is unjustly jailed! But Paul lived what he taught, and he challenged believers—then and now—to strive for those characteristics, as well.

# UNDERSTANDING YOUR KIDS

A lot of Christian kids grow up thinking it's wrong to get angry. But the truth is, anger is a healthy human emotion. Depending on the cause of the anger, there's often nothing wrong with getting angry. But there is something wrong with expressing our anger in ways that hurt people—including ourselves. Interestingly enough, it also appears to be just as harmful in the long run to try to stifle and deny anger as it is to vent it in rage.

Younger kids will often burst into tears and stomp their feet when conflict gives way to anger. Kids in the primary years may resort to hitting and name-calling. Older elementary kids may use sarcasm and mockery to vent their feelings.

Kids of all ages can learn simple techniques to help bring their feelings under control and work toward a solution. Slammed doors and name-calling don't make for positive change. An honest, open discussion of the source of conflict does.

# The Lesson ATTENTION GRABBER

### Caution: Explosives!

Take kids outside to an open, grassy area or a parking lot and form a circle. Toss a can of soft drink up in the air and catch it yourself. As you catch the can, finish the sentence: "It really makes me mad when..." Then toss the can to a student across the circle. Have that student finish the same sentence and then toss the can to another person. If you have lots of small children, you might want to have kids just hand the can to them.

Keep going until everyone in the class has caught the can and told what makes him or her mad. If the can gets dropped and well shaken up in the process, so much the better. If the can hits the ground and pops open before you finish, skip to the second question below.

Have the last person toss the can back to you. Shake it a little and ask:

● **What's going to happen when I open this can?** (It's going to explode; it'll make a big mess.)

Go ahead and open the can, being careful to aim the spray away from yourself and toward the empty center of the circle. Kids will probably scream in delight as the soft drink blasts from the container.

Ask:

● **Why did the can blow up like this?** (Because we tossed it around.)

● **How is this like what happens when people get angry?** (They get so mad they blow up and yell at everyone around them.)

● **When have you ever gotten angry and blown up like this?** Allow several kids to reply.

● **Does blowing your top make things better? Why or why not?** (Not usually, it just makes others mad at me; yes, I feel better.)

Say: **It never really pays to blow your top. It's a lot smarter to learn how to handle conflicts and arguments so things get better—not worse. Today's Bible story is about a man who knew how to do that. Let's see what we can learn from him.**

## BIBLE STUDY

**Keeping the Peace (Genesis 13:1-18)**

Lead children inside.

Say: **First we have to set up the scene for this story. Let's form two groups. Count off by twos.**

**The ones are over here—you're Abraham's group. The twos stand on this side of the room. You're Lot's group.**

117

Ask for a volunteer from each group—one to play the role of Abraham, and the other to play the role of Lot. Have the two volunteers stand face to face, with their feet planted and their arms crossed.

Say: **The Bible says both Abraham and Lot were very wealthy. They had lots of money and flocks and herds and tents. Let's have two people from each group put their hands together over their heads in an arch to make a tent.**

**Now I need some people to be the flocks—drop down on all fours and say "baa."** Have all but two or three kids remaining in each group be the sheep.

Then say: **Good! Now these flocks need some shepherds. So the rest of you are shepherds. Pretend you have a staff in one hand.**

**Now listen and do your part as I tell the story. The tents will move when I say so, the sheep will "baa" when I mention sheep, the shepherds will do what I say in the story, and Abraham and Lot will act out their parts and move their lips when they're supposed to be talking. Listen carefully for when you're supposed to move and what you're supposed to do. Is everybody ready?**

Read the story Abraham and Lot on page 119, pausing to allow kids to do their actions.

Have all your kids give themselves a round of applause. Then ask:

● **Why didn't Abraham fight for his rights?** (He didn't want a fight; he cared more about keeping the peace than getting the good land.)

● **What happened to Abraham because he acted unselfishly?** (God blessed him and promised to give him the whole land.)

● **What was more important to Abraham than getting his own way?** (Keeping the peace.)

● **What advice do you think Abraham would give us about settling arguments?** (Think about the other person's feelings; don't always insist on your rights; be willing to compromise.)

List kids' responses on newsprint taped to the wall.

Then say: **Those are all really good ideas. And they work, too. But when there's a problem, we don't always think about the other guy's feelings. We think about our rights and what we want and how we feel and BOOM!— suddenly we're in the middle of a big fight.**

# Abraham and Lot

God told Abraham and his nephew Lot to move from Egypt to the land of Canaan. Abraham and Lot were both very wealthy men, so they had to move their tents and their sheep and their shepherds. When they got to the place called Bethel, Abraham bowed down and worshiped the Lord.

But soon a problem arose. Abraham and Lot had so many sheep there wasn't enough grass and water to go around. The sheep got very thirsty. Abraham's shepherds and Lot's shepherds started fighting.

"Our master is greater than your master, so move your sheep," Abraham's shepherds said.

"But we got here first, so go find water somewhere else," Lot's shepherds argued.

Meanwhile, the poor sheep got thirstier and thirstier. Abraham and Lot were sitting in their tents when they heard about their shepherds fighting. They both shook their heads and then went out to talk things over.

Abraham said: "Let's not quarrel about this. After all, we're family. Look over this whole land and choose the part where you want to live. If you go one way, I'll go the other."

Abraham really didn't have to be so nice. Because he was older, he was the boss and could have chosen first. But Abraham trusted God to work things out, so he let Lot make the first choice.

Lot looked to the right and to the left. On one side was a valley with lots of grass and water and even some cities. On the other side stood rugged mountains and wilderness.

Lot said: "I'll take the plain. You take the mountains."

So Lot moved his tents and his sheep and his shepherds toward the city in the valley. Abraham moved his tents and his sheep and his shepherds toward the mountains.

Abraham kept the peace, even though it meant living in rougher territory. God blessed Abraham and promised to give him the whole land. Lot, who chose selfishly, got in big trouble moving to the wicked city and barely escaped with his life!

## LIFE APPLICATION

**Marshmallow Madness**

Say: **Let's have a big fight right now—just to see what it feels like.**

Have kids help you lay a masking tape line down the middle of the room. Have Abraham's group form a team on one side of the line, and Lot's group form a team on the other. Give each team a bag of large marshmallows.

Say: **Okay, you guys are really mad at each other—so mad you're ready to throw marshmallows! So go ahead and explode. Throw all the marshmallows you can at the other team. When you get hit by a marshmallow, throw it right back at the other team. When I call time, the team with the most marshmallows on its side loses. Ready? Go!**

Call time after about two minutes. Count up the marshmallows on each side and declare the winners and losers.

Then ask:

● **How does it feel to be a winner?** (Great!)

● **How does it feel to be a loser?** (Awful.)

● **How was this marshmallow war like a real argument?** (We fought as hard as we could; we tried to hurt them more than they hurt us; it got kind of out of control.)

● **How was it different from a real argument?** (Nobody really got hurt; we're not really mad at each other; everyone is still friends.)

● **How could we have made this come out with no winners or losers?** Kids may or may not realize that if no one had thrown any marshmallows, both teams would have had the same number, and no one would have won or lost.

Say: **It's fun throwing marshmallows back and forth. But it's not fun when we let our anger explode and start exchanging hurtful words. God wants us to be peacemakers, even if it means giving up some of our rights as Abraham did.**

## COMMITMENT

**Pointers for Peace**

Give kids each a photocopy of the "Peacemaker Certificate" handout (p. 122) and a pencil. Ask a volunteer to read the Bible passage aloud. Then have kids take turns reading the peacemaking pointers in the corners. Discuss how each one can help kids control their anger and start working toward a peaceful solution.

Then have volunteers role play as many of the following situations as you have time for. Do each role-play twice. The first time, have kids get angry and shout. The second time, have the kids use the advice on the certificate to work toward a peaceful resolution.

Here are the situations:

● **Your brother borrowed your bicycle. The next day you go to ride it and discover it has a flat tire.**

● **Someone accidentally runs into you in the hall at school and knocks your books all over the floor.**

● **You didn't hang up your clothes, and your mom is really angry with you.**

● **Your sister is playing loud music on her boom box and it's driving you crazy.**

● **Your younger brother knocked over and destroyed your latest Lego creation.**

After the role-plays, say:

**These peacemaking ideas really work! They worked for Abraham, and they can work for you. If you're ready to work at being a peacemaker, sign your name on your certificate.**

**TEACHER TIP**

Kids don't necessarily have to take parts that match their age. It's fun for the younger ones to role play being a teenager or a parent.

# CLOSING

**People at Peace**

Gather kids in a circle and have them put their arms around each other's shoulders. Close with prayer, asking God to help kids work for peace and trust the outcome to him.

As kids leave, encourage them to share the peacemaking ideas on their certificates with their families.

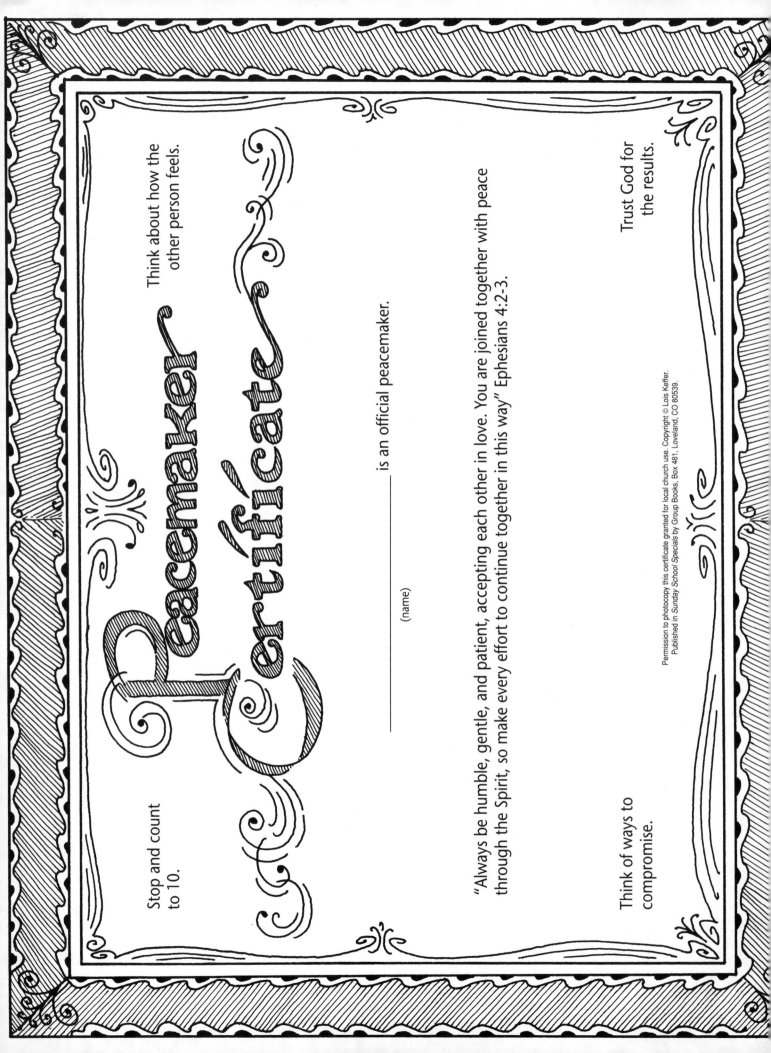

# Peacemaker Certificate

Stop and count to 10.

Think about how the other person feels.

_____ is an official peacemaker.

(name)

"Always be humble, gentle, and patient, accepting each other in love. You are joined together with peace through the Spirit, so make every effort to continue together in this way" Ephesians 4:2-3.

Trust God for the results.

Think of ways to compromise.

# More Children's Ministry Resources From...
# *Group*®

## *5-Minute Messages for Children*

*Donald Hinchey*

Captivate and challenge young listeners—with 52 Bible-based sermons just for them. Each creative message uses language kids readily understand—so you'll teach meaningful lessons on Bible-based topics such as ...

- God's love
- Faith
- Putting God first
- Forgiveness

... and dozens of other topics. Plus, each talk uses involving activities to grab and hold kids' attention—so they'll remember the truths you present.

You'll also get seasonal ideas for helping children understand the meaning of...

- Advent
- Easter
- Pentecost
- Christmas

... and other important days. You'll use these lessons for children's moments in Sunday worship—or at camps, retreats, and other special events.

ISBN 1-55945-030-4

## *6-Minute Messages for Children*

*Donald Hinchey*

Here's the perfect resource for the busy children's worker who wants to give an excellent children's devotion without all the work. Now it's easy to deliver meaningful children's messages that kids enjoy and remember. Instead of a simple object-lesson lecture...

- each message uses a concrete experience,
- kids are encouraged to share their feelings,
- many lessons include a skit or game, and
- some messages suggest simple take-home memory aids.

Each message is based on an important Christian theme and Bible text with a helpful list of needed supplies. Great for Sunday school opening exercises, children's church, midweek meetings... any time you need a quick children's devotion.

ISBN 1-55945-170-X

## *Fidget Busters*

### *101 Quick Attention-Getters for Children's Ministry*

*Jolene L. Roehlkepartain*

Teach children more—by keeping them focused on your lesson. Be ready whenever short attention spans give way to wiggles and squirms. Simply grab one of these quick activities—get kids up and moving—then bring them back to the lesson ready to learn!

You'll get lively, age-appropriate ideas that...

- Require little or no preparation,
- Get kids excited about learning,
- Burn up excess energy, and
- Help you take—and keep—control of your group

... as they perk up kids' interest... and keep them coming back to your class for more. Help your kids enjoy learning—and build closeness in your group—with these creative activities carefully planned for children from preschool through the sixth grade.

ISBN 1-55945-058-4

---

Available at your local Christian bookstore. Or write Group Publishing, Inc., Box 485, Loveland, CO 80539.

# More Creative Programming Resources...

## *Teaching Children in the Church*

*Video training series*

Equip teachers for Sunday school, Bible study, children's church, VBS, and other classroom activities with children from preschool through the sixth grade. In just two hours of training, your teachers will discover how to...

- Teach active classes that whet kids' hunger for learning,
- Help young people apply Scripture to their daily lives,
- Handle classroom discipline with confidence, and
- Guide young people into lasting relationships with God.

Plus, adults will get specific skills for working with the age group they teach—such as...

- Techniques for explaining abstract concepts in ways preschool and kindergarten kids understand,
- Ways to teach first- and second-graders more—by taking advantage of their need for activity,
- How to help third- and fourth-graders learn by using their developing verbal skills, and
- Ideas for teaching lessons that appeal to the developing maturity of fifth- and sixth-graders.

You'll get 120 minutes of training on 5 quality videos—and a leaders guide filled with time-saving meeting plans you'll use to train teachers for years to come.

ISBN 1-55945-279-X

## *Esteem Builders for Children's Ministry*

Now Sunday school teachers have an effective new resource to help children from preschool through sixth grade learn to affirm and serve other children and adults. You'll get 101 esteem-building activities, including games, art projects, and service projects that will help children...

- develop their own positive self-image,
- understand how God views them as his creations,
- appreciate the God-given differences between people, and
- learn how to affirm others by their words and actions.

Each activity is easy to prepare; just gather a few easy-to-find supplies or photocopy one of the handouts included in the book. Makes a great opening exercise as children arrive in class.

ISBN 1-55945-174-2

## *Children's Ministry Care Cards*®

Inspire and affirm your kids. Each card has a fun cartoon to capture children's interest—and an easy-to-understand Bible verse to teach young people about God.

### Affirmations
Uplifting messages to brighten a child's day and encourage his or her faith.
ISBN 1-55945-181-5

### Birthday Greetings
Make your kids feel special—and boost their self-esteem.
ISBN 1-55945-182-3

Available at your local Christian bookstore. Or write Group Publishing, Inc., Box 485, Loveland, CO 80539.

# Add Fun and Creativity to Your Ministry...

## *Making Scripture Stick*

*Lisa Flinn & Barbara Younger*

Discover 52 unforgettable Bible verse adventures for children in grades 1-5. You'll use creative, hands-on learning techniques that draw kids into a world of imagination, discovery, and creative interaction. Bible verses come alive with these active, fun adventures as kids...

- make paper tambourines and use them to create a new song of praise (Psalm 150:4),
- run finger races and discuss the challenges that Christians face (Hebrews 12:1),
- blow bubbles and see that bubbles last an instant while God's love is forever (Psalm 90:2), and
- make a foot-paint footprint banner and see how God watches their every step (Job 31:4).

The easy-to-prepare lessons feature a simple format, clear directions, inexpensive materials, reproducible handouts, and a wide variety of exciting activities. And follow-up discussions make the Bible messages stick!

ISBN 1–55945–093-2

## *Lively Bible Lessons*

You can make creative teaching a snap with these 20 complete children's Bible lessons for each age level. Lively is better, because kids learn more. Each lesson has at least six child-size activities including easy-to-do crafts, action songs, attention-grabbing games and snacks that reinforce the message. Plus, innovative new lessons are included to celebrate holidays like Valentine's Day, Easter, Thanksgiving, and Christmas. Just read the simple instructions, gather a few easy-to-find supplies, and you're ready to go!

| **Preschoolers** | ISBN 1-55945-067-3 | **Grades K-3** | ISBN 1-55945-074-6 |
| **Kindergarten** | ISBN 1-55945-097-5 | **Grades 1-2** | ISBN 1-55945-098-3 |

## *Quick Games for Children's Ministry*

Discover 100 active, creative games for kids from preschool through sixth grade. More than just filling time, you'll use these games to...

- increase Bible knowledge,
- teach teamwork,
- reinforce your lesson,
- build group unity, and
- have fun!

Each game has been field-tested by children's workers from across the country. Plus, you'll appreciate how quick and easy these games are to prepare—with few or no supplies needed! Perfect for use in Sunday school, vacation Bible school, children's church, summer camp—wherever you have a group of kids.

ISBN 1-55945-157-2

Available at your local Christian bookstore. Or write Group Publishing, Inc., Box 485, Loveland, CO 80539.